Introduction

Twenty-first century students work to improve their ability to proficiently and independently read a wide range of complex texts from various content areas. *Lincoln Empowered Literature Collection* is a compilation of literature that provides informational texts, essays, newspaper articles, fables, legends, poetry, short stories, plays, persuasive letters, business letters, diary and journal entries, and more to students learning to read and students reading to learn alike. Even at a young age, students who engage in the careful, meaningful reading of a variety of works develop their ability to:

- Evaluate texts for story elements, literary devices, and/or text features.
- Construct effective arguments based on the content read.
- Discern authors' points of view.
- Ask questions.
- Build vocabulary.
- Gain general and content-specific knowledge.
- Build a stronger worldview through exposure to cultural and era-specific pieces.

This book's contents include all literary pieces used in Empowered courses for one grade level. For easy access, the texts are given in the order in which they appear in Empowered courses.

This collection aligns with the most recent course content at the time of printing.

Contents

Water the Good Ones and Tomatoes 1
Granny's Little Helper 3
A Long Wagon Ride 4
The Clever Rabbit 5
Hippos Stay Cool 6
Studying the Universe 7
The Assembly Line 8
Ruby's First Day of School 9
Photographing Nature 10
Fire in the Kitchen! 11
Raising Money 13
Where Is the Tablet? 14
A Spanish Meal 15
Oscar and the Three Otters 17
Wiffle Wheels 18
Sally's First Pet 19
The Farmers' Market 21
Lily and Grandma 22
Apple Tree Swing 24
The New Girl 26
Otis and the Tummy Ache 27
Two Are Better Than One 29
Broadway and the Missing Hat 31
Fun at the Fair 33
A Horse Named Bee 34
A Birthday Surprise 35
Chavez and the Grape Boycott 37

Albert Einstein 39
Night Flight 40
An American Hero 42
The Dragons' Festival of Wind 43
Jane Goodall 45
Brush Your Teeth 46
Clever Octopus 47
Animal Habitats 48
The Value of Exercise 49
How to Bathe Your Dog 50
A Strong Body 51
Aerobic Exercise 52
The Large Dog 53
The Promise 54
Take Care of Your Body 55
Lemonade for Sale 56
Railroad Songs 57
Tracks Across America 59
Amelia Earhart 61
The Wright Brothers 63
King and the Bus Boycott 65
Hedgehogs 67
Farm Art 68
I Need a Dog 70
Thanking Veterans 71
You Should Exercise 72
Baby Blue Whale 73

Title	Page
Gary's Gift	74
A Day with Dicky	75
Flip, Flop, Thump	76
Limerick Collection	78
Sampan	79
A Wildflower Surprise	80
Neighborhoods: Where Will You Live?	82
Force and Motion at Play	83
'Twas the Morning of Earth Day	84
"I Asked My Mother" and "Way Down South"	85
April's Trick	86
Ladybug, Ladybug	87
Fly Away, Fly Away	88
Pumpkins	89
I Had a Little Pig	90
Silly Things	91
Teddy Bear, Teddy Bear	92
The Squirrel	93
Late for School!	94
The Snake	95
My Perfect Weekend	96
July	98
Hush, Little Baby	99
The New-England Boy's Song about Thanksgiving Day	100
The Swing	102
The Pasture	103
Navajo Chief's Blankets	104
Owl Facts	105
Colossal Crazy Horse	106
What Will a Magnet Attract?	108
A Strong Leader	110
Coquís and Other Frogs	111
Leopard Sharks	112
Run, Bird, Run!	113
Giant Pandas	114
The Golden Fish	115
The Goose That Laid Golden Eggs	117
A Bell for the Cat	118
The Pancake	119
The Tortoise and the Eagle	121
The Fox and the Stork	123
The Rabbit That Ran Away	124
The Little People	126
The Frog Prince	128
The Monkey and the Crocodile	130
The Tiger and the Big Wind	132
The Four Musicians	134
The Shoemaker and the Elves	136
Paper Airplane	138
Make a Necklace	140
An Experiment	141
Bird in a Cage	142
Pennsylvania Facts	143
Fun with Magnets	144
Write a Postcard	145
Example Dictionary Page	146
Example Glossary	147
The Threat to Polar Bears	148

Parts of an Apple 150

Saucy Apple Pudding 152

Instructions for Cooking 153

Make a Stamp for Printing 154

The Best Day of the Weekend 155

Plants Aplenty 156

The Pumpkin Patch 158

A Special Machine 159

A Forest Food Chain 160

Doctor's Office 161

Beavers at Work 162

The Life of a Worker Bee 163

Freshwater Lakes 164

Making a New Lake 165

Learning from Pictures 166

What Cameras Can Do 167

A Promise and a Prince 168

The Boy Who Cried Wolf 170

The Patient Wolf 171

Big Pig and the Pancake 172

How the Princess Learned to Laugh 173

Two Princes 175

A Famous Statue 176

A Gift of Art 177

How a Food Chain Works 178

Food Chain Facts 179

Earthworms in the Garden 180

LINCOLN EMPOWERED
LITERATURE
COLLECTION

ENGLISH LANGUAGE ARTS
2

LINCOLN EMPOWERED

Water the Good Ones and Tomatoes

written by Steve Karscig
illustrated by Sean Patrick Kennedy

Daddy was watering the ferns. Mommy was fixing lunch in the kitchen. Berta was watching her younger brother, Zack, in the backyard. Zack could not help but glare at Berta. He felt she always pushed him in the wrong direction and made him get in trouble. All Zack wanted to do was help Daddy water the ferns in the backyard. Daddy did not want Zack to get dirty. Daddy asked Berta to watch him. Zack thought Berta got all the good attention.

While Daddy was busy watering and Mommy was not looking, Berta picked up a handful of cherry tomatoes from the basket by the porch. Zack gave her a dirty look, knowing Berta was going to throw them. Before Zack could say a word, Berta threw a handful of cherry tomatoes right at his face.

"There, Daddy! Did you see what she did?"

"What? Who did?" Daddy replied.

"Berta!" Zack cried. "She threw tomatoes at me to stir me up and get me in trouble."

Daddy looked at Berta. She just stood there in her skirt, spinning around and looking innocent. Poor Zack just sat there with a few small tomatoes around him. Just then, Mommy called from the kitchen for Daddy's help. Daddy set the hose down and walked in the house.

Zack looked closely at the hose flooding the dirt by the ferns. He looked back at Berta. Zack thought it was his turn to be mean to his older sister. He did not care if he got in trouble again. Zack picked up the hose and turned it on Berta. Berta screamed and ran into the house. She stood there in the kitchen dripping wet. Mommy and Daddy stared at her.

"Zack squirted me with the hose," she cried. "I am tired of him always being so mean to me!"

"Well, Berta," Daddy said, "perhaps you should not have thrown the tomatoes at him." Daddy called for Zack. "Zack, come in the kitchen."

Zack arrived in the kitchen just as wet as Berta. "I'm sorry, Berta," he said. "Daddy, it was my fault."

"Why are you wet, Zack?" Daddy asked.

"I figured that Berta would not get in all the trouble if I was also wet," Zack said.

Berta looked at her brother and smiled. "I'm sorry, Zack. I just wanted Mommy and Daddy to think I was the good one. I was wrong. What I did was bad."

"You are both good ones," Mommy said, "but no more of this fighting. Lunch is ready. Help me carry it out to the picnic table. Then, the both of you go and dry off."

After Zack and Berta placed lunch on the table, Daddy called their names. When they turned to look, Daddy squirted all three of them with the hose, including Mommy. Mommy ran to the basket of cherry tomatoes, picked some up, and threw them at Daddy. They all ran around the yard and laughed.

Granny's Little Helper

Carlos's mom dropped him off at Granny's house. Carlos rang Granny's doorbell. Granny opened the door with a big smile. "Hi, Carlos!" she said. "Would you like to be my little helper today?" asked Granny. Carlos smiled and nodded.

Carlos walked into Granny's house. Granny asked him to help wash dishes. Carlos smiled and filled the sink with soapy water. He used a sponge to wipe the dishes. But then a plate slipped out of his hands. "Uh oh," Carlos said. The plate crashed onto the floor and broke.

"Oh, that's okay, Carlos," said Granny. She used a broom to sweep away the glass. Carlos felt awful. "There is a basket of clothes in the laundry room," Granny said. "Can you toss them into the washing machine, please?" Carlos said yes. He put all the clothes into the machine. But then he saw a box of laundry soap.

"I know," thought Carlos, "I'll surprise Granny by helping her even more. I'll put soap into the machine with the clothes." Carlos thought this would save Granny time. But he didn't tell Granny that he added soap. So, later, she added more soap! Soon, bubbles started pouring out of the washing machine. The bubbles filled the entire house! Granny had to mop up all the bubbles.

Later, when Carlos's mom came over, she asked Granny if Carlos had been a good little helper. "Of course!" said Granny with a wink.

A Long Wagon Ride

I was nervous about moving to a new place. It was far across the country. Papa said it would take us months to get there. We had to travel in a wagon. I wished there were a faster way to travel.

I had to get ready for the long wagon ride. I went to the well to get a bucket of water so we would have something to drink. I picked some berries off the bush so we would have more food to eat. I went inside our log cabin one last time. I had to leave many things behind. There was not a lot of room in the wagon. I took one book and read it by the candlelight.

"Lizzie, time to go!" said Mama.

I wanted to read my book some more, but Mama blew out the candle. I said goodbye to the cabin and went to sit in the wagon.

The wagon we rode in had tents of thick cloth over the top. Horses and mules pulled us along. The trails were very dusty and bumpy. At night, it was really cold. We stopped and built a fire. We sat by the fire and ate.

After five months, we finally made it to the new town. It was a long wagon ride. Now, Papa had to build us a new house out of wood.

The Clever Rabbit

Wolf sat under a big yellow moon one night. His stomach growled with hunger. Just then, he saw Rabbit hurrying to her nest. So Wolf blocked the path. He spoke to Rabbit in a sweet voice. "Rabbit, you sure look nice tonight. How about we take a nice little walk together?"

Rabbit tried to run past Wolf. "Don't move!" snapped Wolf. "I'm hungry, and you look like a tasty meal."

Rabbit said, "Why, Mr. Wolf, I am so little and just skin and bones! But I can show you where to get a big chunk of cheese. Follow me."

Wolf was too hungry to say no. He walked with Rabbit until they came to a well. Wolf looked down and saw a large round yellow piece of cheese floating in the water. He leaned into the well to gobble up the cheese. But he lost his balance and fell into the well.

Rabbit chuckled. With the help of the full moon, she tricked the wolf.

Hippos Stay Cool

A hippopotamus, or hippo, spends a lot of time in the water. The hippo lives in Africa, where the weather is hot. Spending time in the water helps keep the hippo cool. The hippo can spend up to 16 hours in the water. That's a long time!

The hippo's eyes, ears, and nose are on top of its head. This means that the hippo can see, hear, and breathe while it stays cool in the water. It also has special eye coverings. These coverings help protect the hippo's eyes so it can see clearly underwater. The hippo can stay underwater and hold its breath for as long as five minutes.

The hippo only lives in water that is not deep. It moves in the water by pushing its body off the ground or rocks in the water. The hippo uses its webbed feet to help it move through the water.

The hippo may want to stay in the water all day, but it has to go on land sometimes to find food. The hippo will eat grass, and then it will go back in the water when it is finished eating.

Studying the Universe

When Neil deGrasse Tyson was nine years old, he went to the Hayden Planetarium in New York City. A planetarium is a place where people can learn about space. At a planetarium, you can learn about the planets and our star, the sun. You can also learn about other stars. Visiting the planetarium sparked his interest. Tyson wanted to learn more about the universe.

Tyson studied hard and became an astrophysicist. Astrophysicists study space. Tyson also wrote articles for science magazines. He published science books. In 1995, Tyson went to work at the Hayden Planetarium. Now, he's the person in charge there.

Tyson is a very good teacher. He explains even hard science topics in a way that is easy to understand. He's helped many people learn about the universe. In 2014, he hosted a television show on TV. It was called *Cosmos*. About 135 million people around the world watched the show. Tyson was able to teach millions of people about the universe!

Tyson's *Cosmos* television show had 13 episodes about different space topics.

The Assembly Line

written by Summer York
illustrated by Sean Ricciardi

Henry Ford was working late.
He was at his factory in Michigan.
The Ford Motor Company made cars.

Cars cost a lot of money in the early 1900s.
Few people could buy them.
Ford wanted to make cars cheaper.
Then everyone could buy his cars.

Ford was good at solving problems.
He knew how to fix things.
Ford stared at his drawings.
They showed the Model T.
The Model T was a type of car.

Ford decided to build this car a new way.
He used an assembly line.
Ford taught his workers.
Each worker did one job.
Ford built huge machines to help.
They made parts faster.
The parts sat on a moving belt.
Line workers put the parts together.

At the end of the line, the car was done.

Ford's factory built lots of cars this way.
Many people drove the Model T.
The assembly line is used in most factories today.

Ruby's First Day of School

In Louisiana on November 14, 1960, Ruby Bridges left her home with her mother. They were going to William Frantz Elementary School for Ruby's first day of school in the first grade. But this was no ordinary ride to school. Federal marshals, who are law officers that work for the United States government, drove Ruby and her mother to the school. They did this to protect Ruby and her mother.

Outside the car window, Ruby saw many angry people in the street. Some of the people were holding signs. Some of them were shouting and throwing things. They wanted Ruby to go back home and not go to the school. William Frantz Elementary School had always had only white students. Ruby was the first African American student to attend school there. Many people were angry about this. In Louisiana in 1960, white children and black children were not allowed to attend the same schools. Ruby's parents did not think this was fair, though. They asked a judge to decide if Ruby could attend William Frantz Elementary School. The judge ruled that Ruby could.

Ruby was not afraid of the angry people she saw because she was not sure what was going on. Ruby could tell that her mother was afraid, though. When the car arrived at school, Ruby got out and walked into the school with the federal marshals. She was very brave.

Ruby Bridges on the school steps with the federal marshals

That entire day, Ruby sat in the principal's office with her mother. After many days, Ruby got used to the school, and many people there were nice to her. Ruby's bravery helped other African Americans stand up for their rights later on.

© Evan-Moor Corp. • EMC 2422

Photographing Nature

People make art for many different reasons. Artists can show how they feel about things through their art. Photography is one kind of art. Ansel Adams was a famous American photographer. Adams enjoyed the beauty of nature. He wanted to share that beauty with others.

In the 1940s, Adams was hired by the United States government. People wanted him to take photographs of national parks. Adams took many photographs of the parks.

Adams felt strongly that more of nature should be kept safe. He took pictures of mountains and trees. He took pictures of rocks and rivers. His pictures showed their beauty. Adams talked to people in the government. He wanted them to make more national parks. Today, these areas are kept safe. People can still see these places and enjoy their beauty.

Ansel Adams took this photograph of the Kings Canyon area in California in 1936. With Adams's help, the area became Kings Canyon National Park in 1940.

Fire in the Kitchen!

written by Vincent J. Scotto
illustrated by Dave Rushbrook

Laura and Brent play in the living room. Their mother is cooking dinner. She is making baked chicken and pasta. Laura eats her pasta with tomato sauce. Brent likes to eat his with cheese. They cannot wait to eat!

"When will dinner be ready, Mama?" Laura asks.

"Start to pick up your toys. It will be ready soon," their mother says.

"I'm hungry now!" Brent whines. "I didn't have a snack earlier."

"Chicken takes time to make," their mother explains. "It will be ready when you are finished cleaning up your toys."

Their mother walks to the cabinet. She gets out some tomato sauce for Laura. She gets cheese sauce for Brent. She puts the cans on the counter. Then she checks on the children.

"Are you still playing in here?" their mother asks. "Don't you remember what I said?"

"Laura isn't cleaning!" Brent complains.

"Yes, I am. It is Brent who isn't cleaning!" Laura defends.

"That's enough!" their mother commands. "Both of you—finish up."

Suddenly, the smoke alarm starts beeping in the kitchen. The children yelp. Their mother hurries to the kitchen. The oven is on fire!

"Fire in the kitchen!" their mother calls to them. "Get to the neighbor's house!"

Laura and Brent rush out the front door. Their mother acts quickly. She gets the fire extinguisher from under the sink. She walks toward the burning oven and sprays. The fire is out with only smoke filling the room. "Phew!" she exclaims. "That was close!"

Laura and Brent's mother decides it is safe to get them from the neighbor. She calls her neighbor's house. "The kids can come home now," she says. "Everything is safe again."

Laura and Brent run back home. "Are you all right, Mama?" asks Laura.

"I'm fine, honey," their mother says. "I'm glad you were both so quick to get out of the house. It could have been very dangerous."

"We know, Mama," says Brent. "Safety first!"

"That's right," she agrees.

"We do still have a problem, Mama," Laura says.

"What's that?" she asks.

"What are we going to eat now?" asks Laura.

Brent quickly replies, "It isn't that chicken!"

Raising Money

written by Summer York
illustrated by Sean Patrick Kennedy

Ethan and Allie walked down the street. They were busy that afternoon. They were raising money for band instruments at school. They asked their neighbors for help.

Allie had raised all of her money, but Ethan was not having much luck. He still needed to raise a lot. Allie was helping him.

They went up to the closest house. Ethan knocked on the door. A man opened it.

"I need money for a trumpet. Can I have some?" asked Ethan. The man shook his head. He closed the door.

"Ethan," said Allie, "I see your problem. Is there a nicer way to ask?"

"Oh, I should say 'please'!" he replied. "Let's try here." Ethan knocked on the door of the next house. A short woman opened it.

"Can I please have some money for a trumpet?" Ethan asked. The woman looked confused.

"Where are your parents? Ask them," she said. She closed the door. Ethan frowned.

"I think you should be clearer," Allie told him. They planned what Ethan should say. They went to the third house. Ethan knocked. A woman with a round face opened it.

"Hello!" said Ethan brightly. "I am raising money to play the trumpet at school. Any amount you can give would help. Would you please donate?" The woman gave Ethan ten dollars! He thanked her, and they left.

"Allie, it worked!" Ethan said. "That was the clearest and nicest way to ask."

Where Is the Tablet?

It was a rainy, cloudy day. Avery felt sad that he couldn't go outside to play. He thought about what he could do inside the house that would be fun.

"I know! I can play my favorite game on the tablet!" he thought.

Avery looked in his parents' room for the tablet, but it was not there. He looked under his bed for the tablet, but it was not there. He looked in his toy box, but it was not there either.

Avery ran out of his bedroom, downstairs, and into the kitchen, where his dad was cooking dinner.

"Dad, have you seen the tablet?" asked Avery.

"I'm sorry, Avery, I have not seen it," said his dad.

Then Avery heard some music. It was the music from his favorite tablet game! Avery listened for the music. The sound got louder and louder as he walked toward the family room.

Avery walked into the family room and saw his little sister playing with the tablet. Avery was happy he found it. He decided to play a game on the laptop while his sister used the tablet.

A Spanish Meal

written by Vincent J. Scotto
illustrated by David Rushbrook

I love it when Grandma comes to visit! She is visiting from Spain. We used to live in Spain. Now we live in Margate. Margate is a city in Florida. It is in the United States. We left Spain because Daddy got a new job. It is so far away from Spain! Grandma can only visit once a year. I love it when she comes because she lets me help cook dinner! Tonight, Grandma arrives from Spain. She is making *paella*. It is a famous Spanish dish. *Paella* is pronounced like this: *pie-yay-ya*.

"Are you ready, Alex?" my grandmother asks. "We need to get started, *niño*."

"I'm ready!" I shout. Grandma likes to call me *niño*. *Niño* means child in Spanish.

"Where are the pots?" she asks.

"They are under the stove," I say. "I will get one for you."

We make the food. It is almost six o'clock in the evening. In Spain, we would eat dinner much later. At six, we would have a snack in Spain. *Paella* would wait until eight or nine. I am so excited to eat it sooner! Grandma heats the oil in the pan. She needs to cook the meat first.

"Is the meat ready, Alex?" Grandma asks.

"All set to go!" I announce. She cooks the meat.

"Now the vegetables, *niño*."

"I have them ready!" I cannot wait until the *paella* is done! Grandma cooks the vegetables.

"We need to be careful, Alex. This part is important." My grandma knows just how to cook it perfectly.

"We need the tomatoes and beans to be just right," Grandma says. "Then we need some water and the special ingredients."

"You got it, Grandma!" I yell with excitement. She cooks and stirs. She is like a master chef. Dinner is almost ready.

Grandma gets the rice. She measures just the right amount. "A little bit more time, *niño*," she tells me.

The *paella* is complete! We all walk to the dinner table. We set the table. Grandma fills my dish. It smells so good! I wait for everyone to get food before I start to eat. It is hard to wait. Grandma gives me a wink and says, "Dig in!"

We all eat. The *paella* is wonderful! It is even better than last year's. Grandma came to visit us in Margate, Florida, today. But tonight, it tastes like we're in Spain!

Oscar and the Three Otters

There once was a family of three otters—Papa Otter, Mama Otter, and Baby Otter. One day, the family left their home on the ocean to go diving deep into the seawater for tasty crabs.

Oscar Octopus knew that the otters were away. So he crept over to their home. Oscar saw three crabs on the table. He took a bite of the biggest crab, but spat it out. It was too chewy. Oscar tried the middle crab, but it was too salty. The smallest crab tasted just right, so Oscar ate it all up. Then he saw three beds made from seaweed. The seaweed in one bed was too long. His arms got twisted up in it. The seaweed in the second bed was too thick. It felt lumpy. The last bed was just right. Oscar crawled in and fell asleep.

Soon, the three otters came home. They saw bits of crab floating on the ocean. Baby's crab was gone! "I wonder what happened," said Papa Otter. "Let's go to sleep. Tomorrow we will try to find out what happened." Papa Otter, Mama Otter, and Baby Otter swam to their beds. Suddenly, Papa Otter and Mama Otter heard Baby Otter scream. They went to his seaweed bed. Baby Otter pointed to Oscar Octopus in his bed!

"Mr. Octopus, why are you in our home?" asked Papa Otter.

"I'm sorry," said Oscar. "I was hungry and tired." Oscar got out of bed. He told the family again that he was sorry, and he swam away quickly.

Wiffle Wheels

written by Summer York
illustrated by Sean Ricciardi

Beth and Evan love recess! They play Wiffle Ball with their friends. They have two teams.

One team bats. The other team fields the soft plastic ball. Beth and Evan are the team captains.

Today is a warm day. Evan's team is winning. Will comes over. He asks to play. Some of the kids laugh.

Will uses a wheelchair. He doesn't have many friends. Sometimes kids tease him. They call him Wheely Willy.

Beth wants to let Will play. But Evan does not.

"You can't play," Evan tells him. "Go away, Wheely Willy!"

Will looks sad. He leaves the playground. Beth is angry.

"You are being mean, Evan," she says. Beth knows that teasing is wrong. It hurts a person's feelings. Evan only laughs.

"I don't want to play with you," Beth says. "You are mean." She starts to walk away. Evan runs after her.

"Beth, I'm sorry," Evan says. "I wasn't trying to be mean. Honest." Then Evan gets an idea.

Beth and Evan go to the gym. They find the gym scooters. They take them to the playground. Then they find Will.

"I'm sorry, Will," Evan says. "Do you want to play our new game? It's called Wiffle Wheels."

The kids sit on the scooters. Now they have wheels, too. Will grins. He is happy. He hits a home run. The kids cheer loudly. Everyone can play Wiffle Wheels!

Sally's First Pet

written by Vincent J. Scotto
illustrated by Mallory Senich

Sally is eager for the weekend. Mommy is taking her to the pet store. Sally will pick out her first pet. She is so excited that she could jump in the air!

The moment has arrived. Sally and Mommy go to the store. Sally looks at the store's sign. It reads: Tina's Pets and More. Bright gold and silver decorations cover the front of the store. Sally cannot wait to go inside and choose her new pet.

"What sort of pet would you like?" asks Mommy.

"I think I need to look around first, Mommy." Sally walks up and down the rows. Each row has different pets. Sally did not know how hard it would be to choose!

First, Sally sees a golden retriever. Her name is Goldie.

"That is much too large, Sally," says Mommy. "Try something a little smaller."

Sally is sad to hear that, but she keeps looking.

Next, Sally finds a cat named Bubbles. She has orange and white spots. Sally thinks she is perfect!

Mommy shakes her head. "That's still too large, my dear. Remember, you need to keep your pet inside your room."

Sally is let down again, but she knows she can find just the right pet.

Then, Sally meets a green iguana named Lizzy. She is sure Mommy will like Lizzy. Lizzy comes in her own glass case!

"This one is close," Mommy says, "but she is still a bit too big. Lizzy would be hard to handle if she ever got loose!"

Sally is crushed again. Will she ever find the right pet?

Just when she is about to give up, Sally finds a pet who is perfect as can be. He is a black and brown hamster named Squeaky. "May I please get this one, Mommy?" Sally begs. "He's so cute! Look at those spots!"

"This one is just right for your room," Mommy says. "It shouldn't be too hard for you to take care of, either. Now we can pick up everything else we need."

Sally and Mommy pick out a cage for Squeaky. They get him a water bottle. They even get him a hamster wheel for exercise. Then they go to the register at the front. Tina, the owner, is waiting for them.

"You are taking my sweet Squeaky?" Tina gasps playfully. "You'd better take good care of him!"

"I promise I will," replies Sally. "He's just the right size for me."

Tina smiles and winks at her.

With that, Sally and Mommy take Squeaky home. Sally cannot wait to start their adventures together!

The Farmers' Market

Maribel hopped into the car. "I can't wait to go to the farmers' market!" she said.

Maribel's dad smiled. "There will be much to look at when we get to the market," he said. "We'd better get going!"

Maribel and her dad arrived at the farmers' market. There were food stands with different treats lined up on the street. The air smelled of cookies and bread. Maribel smiled as she listened to all the families laughing. "It's a nice sunny day to walk around the market," said Maribel's dad. "Let's see what this first stand has."

Maribel looked at the large table. It was full of fruits and vegetables. "These watermelons look good," she said. "Can we buy one, Dad?" Dad paid for the watermelon. Then he and Maribel walked farther down the street.

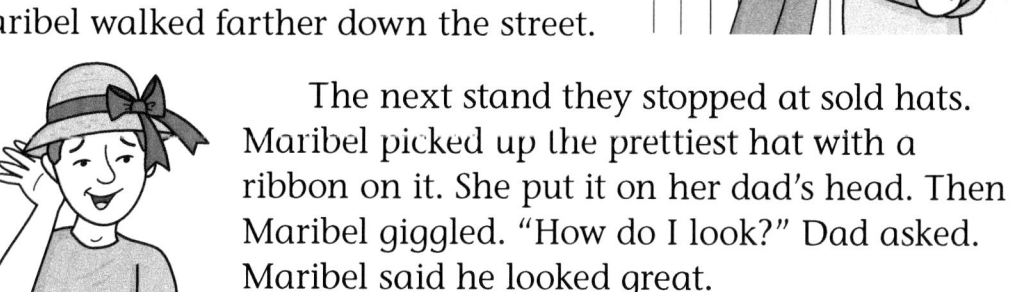

The next stand they stopped at sold hats. Maribel picked up the prettiest hat with a ribbon on it. She put it on her dad's head. Then Maribel giggled. "How do I look?" Dad asked. Maribel said he looked great.

Maribel and her dad spent the rest of the afternoon looking at all the stands. They bought vegetables at a stand. They ate cookies at a different stand. They went home full and happy.

Lily and Grandma

written by Jennifer Tkocs
illustrated by D. Kent Kerr

Lily has a big day planned. Today is Grandparents' Day. She will see her grandma at Oak Manor.

Grandma meets Lily in the lobby. "I'm so glad you are here!" she says. "You will be a big help!"

Lily will help Grandma in the garden. They will plant flowers. The flowers will make the garden look so lovely!

Lily and Grandma put on their gloves. Grandma gives Lily gloves with ladybugs on them.

Grandma shows Lily how to pull weeds. "Put the weeds in this paper bag," Grandma says.

Soon, every weed is gone. "Now it is time to dig!" exclaims Lily. She and Grandma dig small holes in the dirt.

"Place one flower into each hole," Grandma says. They plant the flowers in the garden. Lily likes their bright colors!

"These flowers are so pretty!" she says.

"Yes," Grandma agrees.

Finally, all of the flowers are planted. "What's next?" asks Lily.

"Remember the rocks you painted last weekend?" asks Grandma.

Lily nods. "I painted butterflies and birds on them."

"We can place those rocks along the edges of the garden," says Grandma. "They will be very pretty."

Lily places each rock in the garden. One time, she has to move a worm out of the way first! Soon, the garden is complete.

"Now we will water the plants," Grandma says. Grandma waters each flower. She even waters the little worm!

"Sorry it rained on you!" she tells the worm.

Grandma's neighbor stops by. His name is Mr. Walden. He sees the flowers. "What a great job you two did!" he says. "The garden looks so beautiful."

"I could not have done this without Lily," says Grandma. "She has been such a helper today."

Lily smiles. "This was the best Grandparents' Day ever!"

Apple Tree Swing

I like visiting my grandparents in the fall. This is when we harvest the apples from their tree. This apple tree has been around since my mom was a girl. It's a great old apple tree. Its thick trunk helps it stand strong and tall. The rough bark protects the tree from insects and other things.

A swing hangs from a strong branch of the tree. It is my swing. As you know, branches don't just hold swings. Branches hold apples, and these apples are the best! Some of the apples are ripe now. I know they are ripe because the skin is rosy. The flesh is crispy and sweet.

I cup an apple in my hand and gently push it upward. If it comes off the branch easily, it's ready. If the stem hangs on, it means the apple has more growing to do. Today we picked enough apples for two pies!

Apple Tree Swing, continued

    Grandma's pies are yummy. We had warm apple pie with vanilla ice cream. Grandpa told stories of when Mom was little, swinging on her apple tree swing. Now it's my turn. I like to swing slowly. As I swing, I look up. The sun shines on the leaves, making them bright green. Grandma says that when the leaves are green like that, they are making food. They make food with sunlight, air, and water. The water comes up from the tree's roots. The roots are below the ground. I imagine the roots are like straws, taking water up to the tree.

    I love the apple tree, with its wide trunk and strong branches. I love its thirsty roots and green leaves. I love its rough bark and skinny stems. But most of all, I love its sweet apples and old swing.

The New Girl

Janaya and Krissy were best friends. They liked to do everything together. Janaya was glad to have a best friend like Krissy.

Then one day, a new girl named Deja came to school. She looked sad as she sat by herself at lunch.

"Look at Deja," said Krissy. "She's wearing a shirt with hearts. Only babies wear shirts with hearts," Krissy said as she pointed and laughed at Deja.

"That is not a nice thing to say," said Janaya.

"And look, now she's crying! What a baby!" laughed Krissy.

Janaya grabbed her lunch tray and sat next to Deja.

"I'm sorry Krissy said those mean things. Can we eat lunch together?" asked Janaya.

"OK," said Deja as she wiped her eyes.

Deja and Janaya ate their lunch together. They talked and laughed. Krissy started to feel sad about sitting by herself. She knew that she should have been nice to the new girl. So Krissy softly asked the girls, "Can I sit with you?"

Janaya and Deja looked at Krissy. They made room for her to sit down with them.

Otis and the Tummy Ache

written by Jennifer Tkocs
illustrated by Brian Cibelli

Otis the bear lived in a cave in the forest. He loved his cave. He loved his forest friends. He loved the Forest Fair. But most of all, Otis the bear loved honey.

The Forest Fair was held each summer. Animals of all kinds came to the fair. The squirrels made snacks. The frogs blew up balloons. The rabbits held races. The owls had a spelling bee.

Otis loved the fair. He loved to taste the different foods. He always watched the rabbit races. He and his friends had so much fun.

Last year, Otis was so excited for the fair. Carla the bee had just made her latest batch of honey. It was made just for the fair. Otis bought a whole pot.

The morning of the fair, Otis went to check on his friends. He wanted to make sure they were all coming. He brought his pot of honey to eat.

First, Otis saw Daniel the deer. "Hello, Daniel!" called Otis.

"Hi there, Otis," said Daniel. "How are you today?"

"I am quite fine," said Otis. "Will you come to the fair tonight?"

"Of course," said Daniel. "Say, is that Carla's new honey you have?"

"Indeed it is," said Otis.

"May I have a taste? I haven't tried it yet," said Daniel.

Otis thought for a moment. He did not really want to share his honey. He had only one pot, after all. "Oh, it's not so good," said Otis. "You wouldn't like it anyway."

"Never mind, I suppose," said Daniel. "I'll see you tonight!"

"See you tonight," said Otis. He went on his way.

Next, Otis saw Pepper the rabbit.

"Hi, Otis!" said Pepper, popping out of her burrow.

"Will you come to the fair tonight?" Otis asked.

"I wouldn't miss it for the world!" said Pepper. "By the way, have you got some of Carla's honey?"

"I certainly do," said Otis.

"Oh!" said Pepper. "I would love to taste it. May I have some?"

Otis looked down. He had been eating the honey all day. There was only half a pot left. "Oh, well, I just finished it," he lied.

"Oh, well," said Pepper. "I'll see you tonight!"

Otis went on through the woods, visiting his friends. Each friend noticed the pot of honey, and each one asked for a taste. But Otis did not want to share. The honey was so delicious. He couldn't part with it.

Finally, Otis arrived back at his cave. "There are only a few hours until the fair," he thought. "I should take a small nap."

But then Otis heard his tummy rumble. "Oh, dear," he said. "I do not feel well."

Otis hoped his tummy would get better. He tried to nap. But try as he might, he could not fall asleep. His tummy rumbled and grumbled. He felt sick.

Soon, it was time for the fair. Daniel the deer, Pepper the rabbit, and all of their friends came to Otis's door. "Time to go!" they all called.

But Otis stayed in his bear bed. "Oh, my tummy!" he said.

"What's wrong?" asked Daniel.

"My tummy," said Otis. "My tummy hurts!"

Pepper looked at Daniel. Daniel nodded. "Otis, did you eat all of the fair honey by yourself?" Pepper asked.

Otis was embarrassed. "Yes," he said. "Yes, I did. I ate it all today."

"Why would you eat honey that didn't taste good?" asked Daniel.

Otis had to tell the truth. "Because I lied to you, Daniel," he sighed. "The honey was delicious. It was so yummy that I didn't want to share!"

"You said it was all gone!" said Pepper. "Did you lie to me, too?"

"I did," said Otis. "I am so sorry. I wanted the honey for myself. I did not want to share."

"Oh, Otis, you silly bear," said Pepper. "Now you've gone and given yourself a tummy ache!"

"If you had only shared with us, you wouldn't be so sick!" said Daniel.

Otis put his paws on his tummy. "You are right, my friends. I ate too much honey. I made myself sick. And now I cannot go to the fair! You will have to go without me."

"I'm sorry, Otis," said Pepper. "But maybe next year, you will learn to share. Then you will not get sick. Next year you can join us at the fair."

Two Are Better Than One

written by Vincent Scotto
illustrated by Carys LeRoy

It was the week of Halloween. The class was talking about their plans at the end of the school day. I was talking to my friend Maisy about my costume.

"What will you dress up as?" she asked.

"I am going to be a pirate," I proudly said.

"A girl pirate? What a great idea!" Maisy said.

"What are you going to be?" I asked.

"I am going to be a princess," Maisy told me.

"How cute!" I replied. Yoselin heard us talking. Maisy and I feel sad sometimes after talking to Yoselin.

"Aren't pirates boys? Girls can't be pirates," she said.

"Pirates can be girls or boys," I said.

"Well, it's a dumb idea to be a pirate."

She made me feel sad about my costume. I was really happy about my pirate costume. I wasn't going to be rude back to Yoselin, so I went back to my desk. Maisy followed me and tried to make me feel better.

"Aren't there TV shows with girl pirates?" Maisy asked.

"I think so."

"Girl pirates are just as good as boy pirates," Maisy said.

That made me smile, but I still felt sad. The bell rang to tell us it was time to go home. On my way home, I thought about what Yoselin had said. If Yoselin said that girls can't be pirates, maybe it was true. I walked into my house and asked my mom, "Can I change my costume?"

"What?" she asked.

"I don't want to be a pirate," I told her.

"You were happy to be a pirate this morning. What changed?"

"A girl at school said girls can't be pirates," I told her.

My mom asked me to go with her to the computer. She found websites where we saw tons of girl pirates. I couldn't believe it. "Do you still want to change costumes?" she asked.

"I want to be a pirate again."

"Don't let someone tell you who to be," she explained. "That is your choice."

That night I went to bed happy about my costume. The next morning at school, I was talking with Maisy about our costumes. Yoselin walked by.

"What are you going to be?" I asked.

"I'm going to be a gymnast," said Yoselin.

"Some boys are gymnasts, but no one is stopping you from being one," I said. "Why were you mean to me about being a pirate?"

"I like your costume idea better than mine," she told me.

"Why can't we both be pirates?" I asked Yoselin.

"I guess we could," she said.

"Great!" I said with a smile. "We can be pirate twins."

Yoselin smiled backed. Maisy, Yoselin, and I made a plan to go trick-or-treating together that Friday.

Broadway and the Missing Hat

written by Michael Scotto

Broadway Wannadogood had an unusual job. His job was to pretend. He was an actor. He worked at the Portal Theater. Each night, he went on stage and acted in plays. It was his job to make everyone in Midlandia laugh, cry, and believe.

Broadway was a wonderful actor. After every show, the Midlandians at the Portal Theater told him so.

"Great job!" said Brushy the dentist. "I've never smiled so much in my life!"

"You had me in stitches!" said Sew the tailor.

"My hands hurt from clapping so hard," said grumpy Buck the banker.

"I'm so flattered," replied Broadway. "Thank you." He always made sure to thank his fans.

After each show, the audience went home and Broadway stayed behind to clean up the theater. He swept up the popcorn and straightened the seats. Sometimes, he found things that his guests had left behind by accident.

This was one of those nights. On one chair, Broadway found a hat that had been left behind. "Whose hat could this be?" he wondered. "What a mystery. It looks so familiar."

It certainly was not Broadway's hat. Hats made his bald head feel itchy. "But I'm sure that whoever left this behind wants it back!" he said. "I should figure out whose hat this is and return it."

Broadway thought about all of the Midlandians he knew who wore hats. "I should make a list," he thought. "Tomorrow, I can visit each Midlandian on the list. I'll find the owner of this hat in no time."

Broadway wrote his list and went to bed. In the morning, he went on the hunt!

Broadway's first stop was to see Badge, the police officer. "Sheriff Badge wears a police hat," he thought. "Maybe this is hers."

Broadway found Badge in the town square. She was directing traffic like she did every morning.

"Is this your hat?" asked Broadway.

"Nope," said Badge. "My hat has a star on it so that everyone can tell I am a police officer. But thanks for asking!" Broadway crossed Badge off his list.

Broadway's next stop was at the fire department. He knew that Sparky the firefighter always wore a hat. But the hat did not belong to Sparky, either. "I could never wear this hat," said Sparky. "It's made of straw. It would not be safe when fighting a fire. Safety first, you know!"

Broadway crossed Sparky off the list. Next, Broadway rode over to visit Brick the construction worker. But again, the actor had no luck.

"I wear a hard hat. It is like a bike helmet. It keeps my head safe while I work on my building projects," Brick explained. "This is a soft, floppy hat."

That gave Broadway an idea. "I know who wears a soft, floppy hat!" he said. "Bun the baker!"

Broadway rushed to Bun's bakery. But when he arrived, he could see that the hat did not belong to Bun, either. Bun was already wearing his hat!

"My hat is white and tall," said Bun. He was putting out a tray of fresh muffins to sell. "This hat is brown, round, and short."

Broadway left the bakery quite upset. "I guess I'll never solve this mystery," he thought. As he walked out, Broadway saw Harvest the farmer. Harvest had a cart of fresh fruit he had grown. It was for Bun's bakery.

Broadway looked strangely at Harvest. "Hey, Harvest," he said. "Did you get a haircut?"

"No," said Harvest. "I just normally wear a hat, but I lost it somewhere. I sure hope I find it. I need it to keep the sun off of my neck while I work outside!"

Broadway's eyes lit up. He held out the floppy, brown straw hat. "Here it is!" he cried.

"Oh, great!" shouted Harvest. "Thank you so much for returning it."

Broadway shook his head with a smile. "Of course this hat belongs to you," he said. "I can't believe I did not solve this mystery sooner."

"Don't feel too bad," said Harvest. "You're an actor, not a detective. Let's go back into the bakery, friend. I'll buy you a muffin for your trouble."

Fun at the Fair

written by Vincent Scotto
illustrated by David Rushbrook

The fair is a fun place. Mark, Julie, and Sandy go to the fair. Each of them has a favorite thing to do at the fair. Mark likes to test all of the rides. Julie likes to play games and win prizes. Sandy likes to eat carnival treats. All of the children have fun at the fair.

Mark has a favorite ride at the fair. It is called Quick Silver. Quick Silver is a roller coaster. The cars zip around the track. Mark feels like a king at the top of the ride. The cars go over the hill and down the metal track quickly. Mark thinks that is why it is called Quick Silver. Mark loves the fair.

Julie has a favorite game at the fair. It is called Kick Zone. The zone is a net. To win, you have to kick a ball into the zone three times. Julie kicks the ball as hard as she can into the zone. She misses the zone on the third try. Julie does not give up. Julie always keeps trying until she wins. Julie wins a stuffed animal. Julie loves the fair.

Sandy has a favorite food at the fair. It is called Owen's Fried Onions. She dips the fried onions in Owen's Special Sauce. The fried onions taste better than cake. Sandy wants to work there. Sandy thinks that if she works there she will be allowed to eat all the fried onions she wants! Sandy loves the fair.

Mark, Julie, and Sandy have a fun day at the fair. They go on Mark's favorite ride. They play Julie's favorite game. They eat Sandy's favorite food. These friends love to go to the fair. They will go to the fair again tomorrow. The fair is so much fun!

A Horse Named Bee

written by Jennifer Tkocs
illustrated by Brian Cibelli

Today is an exciting day! Today Maddy and her dad will meet a famous racehorse.

The horse has a funny name. His name is Bee. He was a racing horse. Now he lives at a farm with other horses.

Maddy and Dad arrive at the farm. Maddy hops out of the car. "I can't wait to meet Bee!" she exclaims.

"We must be patient," says Dad. "Bee was a great racehorse. But he is shy around strangers."

They walk up to the fence outside Bee's pasture. "There he is!" says Maddy. She points to a horse standing under an apple tree. It is Bee!

Bee is tall and proud. His coat is shiny and light brown. He lifts his head up and whinnies.

"It's okay," says Maddy. "We are your friends! We brought carrots!"

Maddy holds up a bag of carrots. Bee's ears perk up. He takes a small step forward. Then he takes another step. "Here he comes!" Maddy says.

But Bee is still shy. He steps back below the tree.

"Just wait," Dad tells Maddy. "He'll warm up."

Maddy is disappointed. "I saw Bee race three times," she says. "He was never shy!"

"Bee loves to run," says Dad. "But he gets nervous off the racetrack."

Maddy has an idea. "I love to run, too," she says. "And sometimes I am shy around new people. I know what will help."

Maddy walks to the fence near Bee's barn. "Hi there, friend!" she calls to him. Bee watches her. He is curious.

"Are you ready?" Maddy calls. Then, she takes off running. She runs the length of the fence. She holds up a carrot.

Bee watches from under the tree. Slowly, he puts one hoof out. Then he takes one more step. "That's it, boy!" Maddy tells him.

Maddy runs down the fence to the barn again. Bee takes two more steps. "Dad, you have to run, too!" Maddy says.

Maddy and Dad run together. They run all the way down the fence. This time, Bee understands. He gallops to the edge of the fence.

"That's it, Bee!" says Maddy. "Let's go again!" She and Dad run back to the barn, and Bee runs along with them.

Back and forth they all run. Maddy laughs. Bee skips along like he is doing a dance. "Wow, you really made a friend!" says Dad.

Maddy smiles. She hands Bee a carrot. He happily eats it. "It isn't so hard when you have something in common!"

A Birthday Surprise

written by Jennifer Tkocs
illustrated by Carys LeRoy

Today is Maggie's birthday, but she is sad. Her two best friends were supposed to come over for a party. Yesterday, though, they came down with the chicken pox. Maggie is all alone on her birthday.

Maggie sits down at her desk. She puts her head in her hands. "What a crummy birthday," she says.

"What's crummy about it?" says a voice.

Maggie looks up quickly. "What?" she says. She turns to the doorway. Her door is shut and there is no one there. She looks at her window. There is no one at the window.

"I said, 'what's so crummy about your birthday?'" repeats the voice.

Maggie feels scared. She can't see anyone in her room. She knows her mum's voice and this isn't hers. "Who said that?" she asks aloud. "Who's talking to me?"

"It's me, silly. Over here on your window seat!"

Maggie glances nervously at her window seat. The only thing there is her cat, Linus. "I must be coming down with the chicken pox myself," Maggie mutters. "I thought my cat was talking to me!"

"You thought right," says the voice again. "Isn't it clear? I'm the only one in your room, after all." Linus gracefully leaps off the window seat and onto the floor. "So, let's make this birthday less crummy."

Maggie cannot believe her eyes. "Linus? Is that really you talking?" Maggie thinks hard about any birthday wishes she may have made. "How can I hear you?"

"You really don't know?" asks Linus. "Let's go for a short walk."

Linus flicks his tail toward Maggie's door. Bewildered, Maggie follows. She opens the door to the hallway. Linus leads her to the den.

"See those boxes in the corner? Open the top one. There is something in there," says Linus.

Maggie approaches the stack of boxes and opens the top one. Inside are photos of herself as a baby with her parents. The third one shows a woman Maggie does not recognize. "Who is this?" she asks Linus.

Linus laughs a hearty cat laugh. "Why, Maggie, that is your fairy-aunt Andrea, of course. You don't know her?"

Maggie shakes her head. "No. I've never met her. And I've never seen this photo before."

Linus stretches and leaps onto the desk chair. "You have met her, but not since you were little. She had to go very far away. But before she left, she gave you a gift."

"Where is it?" asks Maggie.

"It's inside of you," says Linus. "Your fairy-aunt Andrea gave you the gift of the Voice of the Animals. On your seventh birthday, you would be able to talk to all animals. You can hear our voices now, as well."

Maggie cannot believe it. "But how do I know it's true?" she asks.

"You hear me, don't you?" asks Linus.

"Yes, but maybe I have a fever. Maybe I am imagining it," says Maggie.

"How old did you turn today?" asks Linus.

"Seven," replies Maggie.

"Open that window," says Linus. "Say hello to the squirrel there on the tree branch."

Hesitantly, Maggie walks to the window. She pushes it up. "Hi, squirrel," she says, feeling foolish.

"Good morning, Maggie!" says the squirrel. "And happy birthday!"

"Thank you," Maggie says. She is still in shock.

"Believe me now?" asks Linus.

Slowly, Maggie nods. "I guess I do. But why me? And how did it happen?"

"There will be plenty of time for explanations," says Linus. "But for now, let's go work on improving this birthday!"

"Okay," says Maggie. She is still unsure of what Linus has told her, but her birthday suddenly seems a little more interesting.

Chavez and the Grape Boycott

Cesar Chavez was born in Yuma, Arizona, in 1927. His family owned a small farm and a grocery store. When Cesar was ten years old, a drought destroyed his family's farm. There was no rain, and the crops dried up.

The family moved to California to start over. They became migrant farm workers. They went from farm to farm looking for work. They never stayed in one place very long. In fact, Cesar attended over 30 schools! In eighth grade, he left school to help his family by picking grapes. Farm work was hard. Workers were paid very little money. Sometimes they had to live in run-down camps without clean water.

Chavez and the Grape Boycott, continued

Cesar Chavez felt the workers should have a better life. He remembered that Dr. Martin Luther King, Jr., had led nonviolent marches. The marches got people to listen. Chavez decided to help the farm workers. Chavez asked the workers to stop working and to march with him. In 1965, they marched to demand fair wages and safe working conditions. Chavez got another idea. He asked people to stop buying grapes. He hoped this boycott would make the grape growers listen.

The boycott and the marches worked. People all over the United States stopped buying grapes. By 1970, the growers finally gave the workers what they wanted. The growers made changes. Some of the changes became laws in California. Cesar was an ordinary man who made big changes happen. Until his death in 1993, Chavez worked to improve the lives of farm workers.

Chavez (front, center) leads a march in Coachella, California, around 1991.

Albert Einstein

written by Summer York
illustrated by Sean Ricciardi

Albert Einstein was a poor student.
But, he grew up to be very smart.

As a boy, Einstein was not a good student.
He liked math and science.
He did not like his strict school, though.
Einstein quit school when he was fifteen.
But he could not find a job.
He knew he needed to learn more.
So he started school again.
Then he worked as a clerk and a teacher.

He wrote about science.
He was starting to discover new things.
Many people read Einstein's work.
His ideas spread.
He became well-known for his ideas.

Einstein did not start as a good student.
But, his discoveries changed the world.

Night Flight

written by Vincent J. Scotto
illustrated by Matthew Casper

During the day, Carla is like a normal little girl. Carla plays on the playground with friends. Carla helps with chores around the house. Carla even brushes her teeth before bed. When Carla's parents go to sleep, she sneaks out of her room. She goes down the steps and out the back door. As soon as no one is looking, Carla jumps up into the air and begins to fly! Tonight, Carla has a busy night planned.

Carla flies to her friend's house. Her friend's name is Jake. Carla picks him up and flies away with him on her back. "Where are we going tonight?" says Jake.

"We will fly to the pyramids in Egypt!"

Carla and Jake arrive in Egypt. Carla lands on top of the first pyramid she finds. The two of them sit near the point at the top for a while.

"This is so cool!" Jake declares. "How did you learn to fly? You never told me."

"Do you remember when we found the well in that field?" Carla asks.

"Of course I remember," Jake says.

"I threw a penny in the well and wished to be able to fly. That night, I started floating in my bed!"

It is getting very late. Carla and Jake decide to fly home. Carla drops off Jake at his house. Jake climbs into his bed. "Will we fly again tomorrow?" Jake asks.

"You bet we will!" Carla announces. She flies away from Jake's bedroom window.

Carla finally arrives at home. She crawls up the stairs in her house and climbs into bed. Suddenly, Carla's mother walks into her bedroom.

"Are you all right, Carla?" she asks. "I heard you coming up the stairs."

"I just wanted a drink," Carla explains. "I'm going back to sleep now."

"I'm sure you were thirsty," Carla's mother says. "Flying all night would make me thirsty, too!"

An American Hero

Long ago in the United States, some people enslaved African people. They called them "slaves." Slaves lived and worked on large farms. They worked hard, but they didn't get paid. They didn't get to choose how to live their lives. Farmers who owned slaves could sell them whenever they wanted. It was a horrible life.

Harriet Tubman was an enslaved African. She lived in Maryland, which was a state in the South. Tubman knew that slaves could be free in northern states. Harriet Tubman wanted to be free, so she secretly ran away. She had to hide because she was in danger. It was a long way to the North. If she were caught, she would be sent back.

Harriet Tubman was born around 1820 and died in 1913.

Harriet Tubman made it to Pennsylvania, a northern state. She was free! But Tubman wanted to help other slaves, too. So she went back to the South to help more slaves leave. She went back and forth many times. Tubman helped almost 300 slaves get to the North. She helped them become free. Today, Tubman is remembered as a great American hero.

The Dragons' Festival of Wind

written by Sarah Marino

In a village high up in the sky, there lives a group of friendly dragons. Their houses, built on clouds, have many shapes and sizes. Some houses are squares, some are triangles, and others are rectangles. All of the houses are very tall, because the dragons who live in them are very big!

Today the dragons are busy in the park. The Festival of Wind is about to begin. The Festival of Wind happens every spring. That is when the dragons blow their strong breath and make wind for the earth. The wind is very important. It pushes the clouds across the sky. The clouds are made of tiny raindrops. As the clouds move in the wind, rain falls to Earth and makes food grow. Without the dragons' help, people would have nothing to eat.

One little dragon named Dina is sad. She is not big enough to make wind with her breath. She is only five years old. She is red and orange and has big green eyes.

Dina asks, "When will I be able to make a wind that moves the clouds? I really want to help."

"Only the biggest dragons can make the wind, Dina," her mommy answers. "Even your daddy does not do it, though he is big and strong."

"That's right," her daddy says. "But don't forget, Dina, we can help in other ways."

This year, the dragons are making special gifts to send to people on Earth. They are making houses for a town that needs them. The houses will be carried into the town by the wind, along with the rain clouds. Dina's family will help to make the houses.

Dina and her family start to build a house. They use rectangles of wood to make the floors. Then they put the walls in. After that, they put a roof on and add a chimney and windows. The house is a square with a triangle roof.

After the houses have been made, the dragon president flies above the crowd. His green scales sparkle in the sun. "Thank you, my fellow dragons, for your hard work," he says. "We will send these houses to Earth with the rain clouds. Many people need these houses, and they also need the rain. Soon, the seven largest dragons will create the first wave of wind."

The biggest dragons walk to the edge of the park. Their footsteps sound like thunder. The dragon president flies over them. In a loud voice, he calls out, "On the count of three, make your wind! One, two, *three*!"

The seven dragons raise their huge heads and move their necks forward. Their mouths open. They blow a huge blast of wind into the clouds. The clouds soar away from the dragon village, down through the sky.

The dragons in the park roar in celebration. The winds have moved the clouds!

Now the families carry the houses they have made. They watch as the seven biggest dragons blow them across the sky.

"That was a good thing you did, Dina," her daddy says as he gives her a hug. "We need to help each other when we are able. I'm very proud of you."

"Thank you, Daddy," says Dina. "I like being a helper. Even if I'm not big enough to make wind, I can help in other ways."

"That's right," her mommy says. "And that's what counts."

Jane Goodall

Jane Goodall was born in England in 1934. When she was one year old, her father gave her a stuffed toy chimpanzee. She loved it! Chimpanzees became her favorite animal. Goodall read *Dr. Dolittle* when she was seven years old. It was a book about a doctor who could talk to animals. Goodall decided she wanted to study wild animals when she grew up. She wanted to be able to talk to animals like Dr. Dolittle.

When she was older, Goodall went to Africa to study wild chimps in Gombe National Park. She learned many things about chimps that no one knew before. Many chimps lived in the park's forests. Goodall watched the chimps closely. She learned their language, called "chimp talk." She watched them play and search for food. She saw them make friends or fight. She learned by watching. She told people what she learned.

Today, Dr. Jane Goodall travels all over the world. She asks people to help chimpanzees. Many forests are being cut down. Some people hunt chimps for food. Goodall works to help keep chimps safe. Goodall believes that when people hurt nature, they hurt themselves. She started the Jane Goodall Institute to protect chimpanzees and their environments.

Brush Your Teeth

Brushing your teeth every day is very important. You should brush your teeth at least twice a day. You should brush your teeth after breakfast and before you go to bed.

When you brush your teeth, you clean food off them. Brushing helps you keep your teeth healthy. When food stays on your teeth for a long time, it can cause your teeth to get holes in them. The holes in your teeth can make your mouth hurt. You should brush your teeth so they won't hurt. If your teeth do start hurting, you should go to the dentist. The dentist can help you keep your teeth clean and healthy.

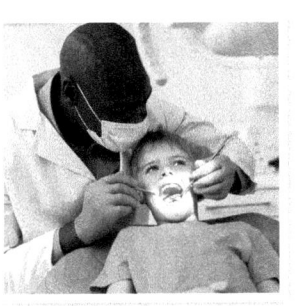

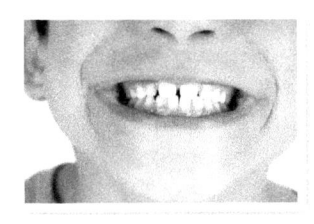

Brushing your teeth can help your breath smell fresh. When food gets stuck between your teeth, it can make your breath smell stinky. Most people do not want to have stinky breath. And fresh breath is a sign that your teeth are healthy. Brushing your teeth gets rid of the food that may be stuck in your teeth.

Brushing also makes your teeth whiter. White teeth are healthy teeth. White, healthy teeth help you have a nice smile. Be good to your teeth, and brush them at least twice a day.

Clever Octopus

An octopus may look scary with its eight long arms and sticky cups. But this sea animal is a yummy treat for sharks and eels, so it must use many tricks to hide and stay safe.

an octopus hiding on the seabed

An octopus hides by making itself look like a pile of rocks or sand. An octopus can change its skin color to brown, black, gray, or orange so it looks like the seabed. It can make its skin look bumpy like a rock or smooth like fine sand. It is hard for sharks and eels to find an octopus that is hiding.

An octopus also uses its ink to stay safe. If a shark or an eel comes too close, the octopus squirts ink. The ink makes the water dark so the shark or eel cannot see. Then the octopus swims away.

Small spaces are good hiding places for an octopus. The animal's body is soft, so it can push itself between rocks or into little holes. Sharks and eels are too big to follow the octopus.

The octopus is a clever animal! It keeps itself safe from enemies that are much bigger than it is.

Animal Habitats

written by Jennifer Tkocs
illustrated by Brian Cibelli

Animals live in many places. Some animals only live in dry places. Some animals live near water. Some animals live under the ground. An animal's home is called its habitat. Let's look at three animal habitats.

Birds build their homes in trees. A bird's home is called a nest. Mother birds build nests. They use sticks and twigs. They look for supplies all day. Then they fly back to the tree and build the nest.

No two bird nests are alike. Some are made with grass and leaves. Some are made with twigs. Birds can even use pieces of string or yarn.

The nest protects the bird's eggs. Soon, the eggs hatch. The baby birds stay in the nest until they can fly. The nest must be in a safe place in the tree. It must be hidden.

Muskrats live in a different habitat. Their home is called a den. Muskrats always live near water. They build their dens with cattails, leaves, and roots.

Muskrat dens have many rooms and tunnels. They build the dens in the water. That helps keep them safe. It also makes eating easier. Muskrats eat plants. They also eat animals.

Some animals make homes under the ground. Rabbits do this. Their homes are called burrows. Rabbits have strong legs for digging. They make holes under the ground. The holes have tunnels between them.

Rabbits like to live in meadows. The ground there is soft. It is easier to dig in soft ground. Living under the ground keeps rabbits safe. Rabbits stay warm in the winter down there.

Animals make many different kinds of homes. Every animal makes a home that fits its life.

The Value of Exercise

written by Jennifer Tkocs
illustrated by Mallory Senich

Every person must care for his or her body. We must eat healthful foods. We must get enough sleep each night. We must see the doctor and the dentist each year. Also, every day, we must all exercise.

Exercise is very important. You should do at least sixty minutes of exercise every day. That might seem like a lot. However, exercise is fun! The time will go by very fast. Let's learn all about exercise.

Exercise makes your muscles strong. That includes your heart. Did you know that your heart is a muscle? Running, dancing, or riding your bike will make your heart strong.

You can find exercise that fits any season. In the summer, swim at your local pool. That will cool you off! In the fall, hike in the woods. The trees will be lovely! In the winter, try something indoors. You could do gymnastics or play hockey or basketball. In the spring, try kickball or maybe even a pony ride.

Exercise is a great way to make friends. Do you like to watch baseball? You could join a baseball or softball team in your town. Your new best friend might be the catcher!

You may feel tired right after exercising. But staying active will give you more energy. You will sleep better at night after a long day of playing. Being in better shape will also make you a better helper. You can walk to the mailbox faster. You can carry more groceries. You might even help your parents with the vacuuming.

After you exercise, you must stretch your muscles. This will keep you from getting hurt. It will make you more flexible. Roll your shoulders. Twist from side to side. Reach up as high as you can. Bend down to touch your toes and stretch your legs.

Whatever you choose to do, make sure you exercise daily. You will be stronger and have more energy. You can make new friends and learn new skills. Best of all, you will take a big step toward staying healthy!

How to Bathe Your Dog

written by Jennifer Tkocs
illustrated by Sean Patrick Kennedy

Just like people, dogs need baths. If you have a dog, you can help give her a bath!

First, gather supplies. You will need some towels. Use a beach towel if your dog is big. You will also need dog shampoo. And most importantly, you will need treats!

Next, prepare the bath. Turn the water on. Make sure it is warm, but not too hot. Your parents can help with this step.

Now, bring your dog into the bathroom. She might be scared of the bath. Tell her that she is a good dog. Give her treats. You can lead her to the bathtub with the treats.

Then, take your dog's collar off. An adult can help with that. Now is a good time to give your dog another treat. Let her know she is a good dog!

You may want to have a grown-up wash her collar while she is in the tub.

Help your dog into the bathtub. If she is big and does not want to go in, a grown-up may need to lift her in.

Once she is in the tub, use the shower hose to coat her with water. Talk to her about how clean and pretty she will be! This will help her stay calm.

Put the dog shampoo on her back. Wash her back, sides, and under her belly. Have her lift her paws up so that you can wash each of them.

Have an adult help to wash her face. Do not put water or shampoo in her eyes and ears!

You can give your dog treats all throughout the bath. It will help her feel happy and distract her from being anxious.

After your dog is all soapy, rinse her off. Make sure all of the soap is gone. If she gets out of the bath with soap on her fur, she may try to lick it.

After your dog is clean, turn off the water. Help your dog out of the tub. Have her stand on a towel. Put the other towel over her like a blanket. Rub the sides to dry her.

At this point, watch out! She will probably want to shake, and you will get wet! Keep rubbing your dog with the towel until she is dry.

Reward her good behavior with another treat. Then put her collar back on. You can finally set her free. Most dogs like to run around after their baths. She will feel clean and happy.

A Strong Body

Your body needs many things to stay healthy. One of those things is exercise. There are many kinds of exercise. You probably get exercise without even thinking about it. You might go for a walk or a run. You might dance, swim, or skip. You might ride a bike or go rollerblading. All of these activities are good for your body.

Dancing is a great way to exercise with your family. Play music you all enjoy and move your body.

Exercise helps your body keep working in the right ways. It makes your heart and other muscles grow stronger. Exercise helps your body turn food into energy. This helps you stay at a healthy weight. Exercise even helps your brain get more oxygen so it can think better. If you exercise each day, it can help you feel your best.

You can set a timer to make sure you exercise for at least 20 minutes.

How much exercise do you need? The experts say children should exercise for 60 minutes each day. You don't have to do it all at one time, however. You could do push-ups in the morning, play tag at recess, then ride your bike after school. It all adds up! Exercise will help you stay healthy and happy.

EMC 3232 • © Evan-Moor Corp.

Aerobic Exercise

Exercise is an important way to keep your body healthy. One kind of exercise is called aerobic exercise. For example, running or walking fast is aerobic exercise.

The word aerobic means "needing oxygen." Your body needs oxygen. When you do aerobic exercise, you breathe in a lot of air. The oxygen from the air goes into your lungs. You can feel your heart beat faster. Your lungs and heart work together. They carry the oxygen through your whole body. The exercise helps your muscles, bones, lungs, and brain.

Running with your friends is a great way to exercise. It is fun, too!

One hour of exercise a day can help you grow strong. Most of the hour should be aerobic exercise. You might play soccer or basketball. Jumping rope will build strong bones. Play on a jungle gym to make your muscles stronger.

You already know that exercise can help your body feel better. But exercise can help your mind feel better, too. It can make you feel happier and forget your troubles. Make time for aerobic exercise today!

You can play many different sports. Playing a sport is a great way to get aerobic exercise.

The Large Dog

My name is Greg. I have two dogs, Buddy and Skipper. Skipper loves to chase cats. Skipper loves to jump into pools of mud and piles of leaves. But Buddy is different. He'd rather sleep in his bed. He doesn't want to run with me or chase his ball. Buddy gets tired when he walks from his bed to his dog bowl.

Dad said Buddy was looking heavy. He was worried about Buddy's health. "Why is it a big deal if Buddy is heavy?" I asked.

Dad said that being heavy can hurt Buddy's joints and bones. He said that being large can make it hard for Buddy to feel comfortable. "You want Buddy to be comfortable, right?" Dad asked me. "Wouldn't you be sad if Buddy was in pain?" I nodded. I love Buddy, so I want him to be healthy and comfortable.

Dad and I took Buddy to the vet. Skipper stayed home. The vet asked, "Are you giving Buddy too much food?" We said no. Then the vet had an idea. "Sometimes dogs just need a change in diet. Try this new dog food," she said. "It's very healthy."

We tried the new food, and it helped a lot. Buddy became smaller. He started running and playing more. Best of all, he seemed happier because he wasn't in any pain. I'm glad we took him to the vet so he could start eating healthier dog food!

The Promise

Ashley played with Ben's cat. Kitty purred because Ashley petted her. "Kitty likes you," said Ben. "I am going to visit my grandma, so I need someone to take care of Kitty. Will you watch Kitty while I am at my grandma's house next week?"

"Sure," said Ashley. She was happy to help.

Ashley gave Kitty food and water each day. Ashley played with Kitty. If Ashley threw a ball of yarn, then Kitty ran after it. Ashley and Kitty had fun together.

On Wednesday, Maria called Ashley. "We're going to the mountains tomorrow," said Maria. "I can bring a friend. Can you go? We can play in the snow!"

Ashley wanted to go. Then she remembered Kitty. Ben would not be back until Saturday. "Sorry, Maria," said Ashley. "I have a promise to keep, so I can't go."

When Ben came home, he thanked Ashley for taking care of Kitty. Ashley felt proud because she kept her promise.

Take Care of Your Body

When you take care of your body, you can learn and grow. You do lots of important things with your body. There are many ways to take care of it.

You can make sure that you get enough sleep. When you sleep, your body rests. Your body needs to rest every day so that it does not get tired quickly when you do things such as going to school and playing with your friends. If you don't sleep enough, you feel tired. You can't run fast or pay attention as well as you usually can. Sleep helps you grow, too.

You can also take care of your body by moving and playing. When you move your body, it gets stronger. The more you move your body, the faster you'll be and the farther you can go. So, next time you ride your bike or play tag, remember that you are doing something good for your body.

To care for your body, eat healthy foods, such as fruits, vegetables, and nuts. These are foods that help you stay healthy and strong.

Take care of your body. That way, you can keep doing all the things that you like to do.

Lemonade for Sale

"I want to buy a skateboard," said Nick. "But I don't have any money. How can I earn some money?" Nick asked his sister Patty.

"I know!" said Patty. "You could sell lemonade along the bike path. If you make a lot of money, can you buy me a new puzzle? I want a puzzle with a cool picture."

"Yes," said Nick. "I'll buy you the best puzzle in the store."

Nick found a big table in the garage. His dad helped him move the table. Patty and her mom made lemonade. Nick and Patty made a big sign. The sign said "Lemonade for Sale." Bike riders saw the sign. Many of them came to the table. They were very thirsty after their bike ride. Some bike riders asked for a cup of ice water.

"Sorry, we only have lemonade to drink," said Nick. "Maybe next time I'll sell water, too."

Soon, all the lemonade was gone. Nick was happy that he made a lot of money selling lemonade.

"Now it's time to go to the toy store!" Nick said to Patty.

"I'm coming with you," Patty told Nick.

Railroad Songs

Railroads in America were built long ago, in the 1800s. Before trains, people traveled by boat or by horse. But rivers would freeze in winter, and horses would get hurt or tired. Trains changed all that. Trains were a new and fast way to travel. Everyone wanted to ride the rails.

Railroad tracks were built all across the country. Men worked hard to make the new tracks. They were told to do it fast. The men sang songs to help the work go faster. Men used a special tool to pound nails, or spikes, into the tracks. The tool was called a spike maul. The spike maul was very heavy. The men pounded all day. They sang railroad songs to forget how tired they were. Many of these songs became American folk songs. Here is one song that the men sang:

I've been working on the railroad
All the livelong day.
I've been working on the railroad
Just to pass the time away.
Can't you hear the whistle blowing?
Rise up so early in the morn!
Can't you hear the captain shouting:
"Dinah, blow your horn!"

Railroad Songs, continued

Here is another song that the railroad workers sang:

♪ *She'll be coming round the mountain when she comes.*
She'll be coming round the mountain when she comes.
She'll be coming round the mountain,
She'll be coming round the mountain,
She'll be coming round the mountain when she comes. ♫

Who do you think the song was about? No one really knows. But here's an idea. Ships and trains are sometimes thought of as women. Maybe "she" was a train. Maybe the crew hoped the train had food and supplies. Or maybe more workers were coming. Now people sing this song in school or at camp. They may have other ideas of who the song is about.

There are many other railroad songs. They tell about the time of the trains. Back then, trains were the fastest way to travel. Now people are in more of a hurry. They travel by car or by plane. Many of the railroads are gone, but we still have the songs to remind us of that time.

Tracks Across America

The transcontinental railroad was built between 1863 and 1869. It changed America forever. It linked the West Coast and the East Coast. The railroad affected many people.

For some people, the railroad was good. Store owners could trade with people far away. They could buy and sell things like fruit, animals, and steel. Before, people traveled from San Francisco to New York City by ship. It took many months and lots of money. By train, it took only three days and not as much money. Thanks to the railroad, trade and travel were faster and less expensive.

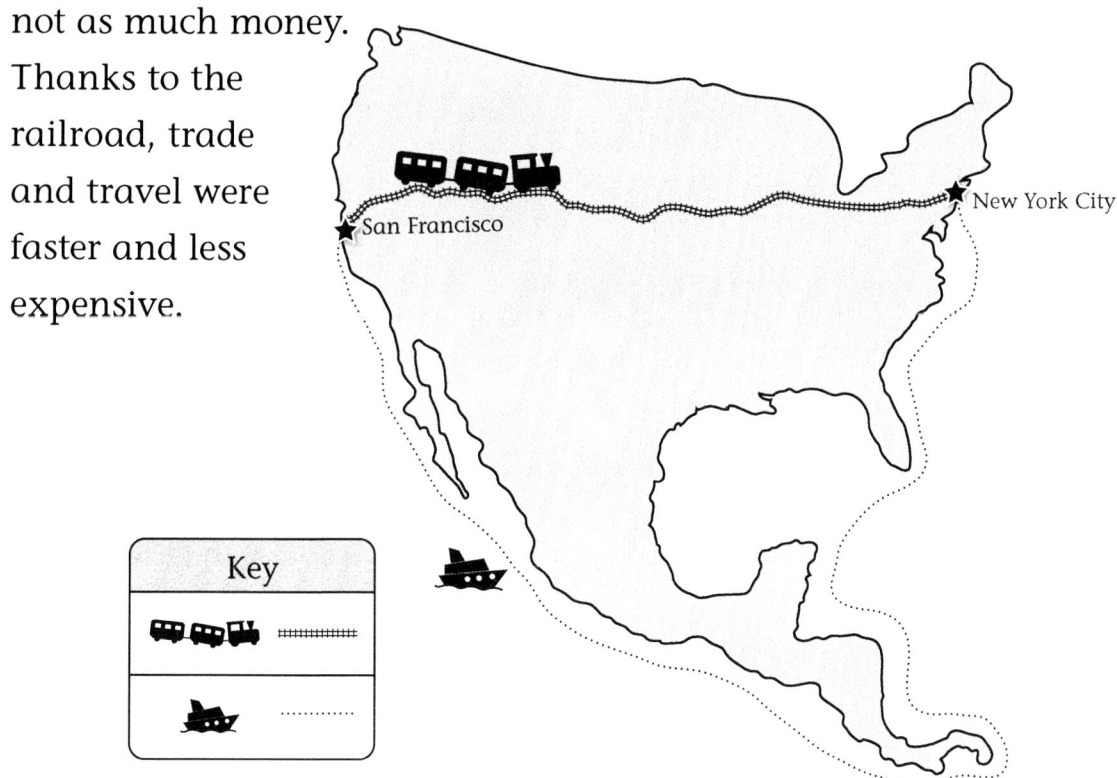

Tracks Across America, continued

For other people, the railroad was bad. Native Americans called the train "the iron horse" because now people were riding trains instead of horses. Native Americans did not like the train. Train tracks cut through their land. Trains destroyed their homes. Train passengers destroyed their food. Native Americans hunted buffalo for food. They only hunted what they needed. There were many buffalo. Then train passengers began shooting the buffalo. In a few years, most of the buffalo were gone.

Native Americans fought back. In the end, though, the railroad won. Native Americans lost their land and their way of life.

The railroad changed the land and the people. For some people, it was a good change. For others, it was not.

Amelia Earhart

written by Jennifer Tkocs
illustrated by David Rushbrook

Amelia Earhart was born in Kansas on July 24, 1897. She was always very curious. Amelia's parents helped her and her sister try many new things.

In Amelia's time, many jobs were held mostly by men. Amelia wanted one of those jobs. She read stories about women who were lawyers, engineers, and movie directors.

Soon, Amelia finished with school. She became a nurse. She worked in Canada during World War I.

Amelia's life changed forever in 1920. She was visiting family in California. She went to an air show. That is a show where pilots do tricks with their planes. She met a pilot named Frank Hawkes. For ten dollars, Amelia got a ride in Frank's plane.

Right away, Amelia knew she was meant to fly. She took flying lessons. She worked hard and saved her money. In less than a year, she bought her own plane.

Soon, Amelia set her first flying record. She flew her plane fourteen thousand feet in the air. She was the first woman to do this. She set another record in 1928. Amelia and two male pilots flew from America to England. She was the first female pilot to cross the Atlantic Ocean.

Amelia took many long flights by herself. In 1932, she flew across the Atlantic again. This time she went alone. She was the first woman to fly across the Atlantic by herself. The weather was icy and windy, but she made a good landing.

In 1935, she flew alone across the Pacific Ocean. She was the first person to do that. She earned many awards and medals. One medal even came from the president.

In 1937, Amelia and her navigator, Fred Noonan, began her longest journey. They planned to fly all the way around the world. Amelia wanted one last great flight.

They only made it most of the way. With just seven thousand miles left, they fell out of contact.

The Navy and Coast Guard searched and searched. But they never found Amelia or her plane. There have been many rumors about what happened. No one knows the truth.

Amelia Earhart is one of the most famous pilots in history. Her story inspired many, even though the ending may never truly be known.

The Wright Brothers

written by Jennifer Tkocs
illustrated by David Rushbrook

Airplanes take off and land every day. Air travel is the second most popular way to travel. But before the 1900s, there were no airplanes. Air travel did not exist.

Everything changed in 1903. It was all thanks to the Wright brothers.

Orville and Wilbur Wright were brothers from Dayton, Ohio. As boys, they loved kites and bicycles. They had a bicycle shop in Dayton. They tried to design newer, better bikes.

Orville and Wilbur also studied aeronautics. That is the science of traveling through the air. There were no airplanes. Still, gliders did exist. The Wright brothers learned as much about gliders as they could. They thought that humans might be able to travel by air.

Orville and Wilbur moved to Kitty Hawk, North Carolina, in 1900. Kitty Hawk was good for flying. It was right next to the ocean. It had strong winds. It had sand for soft and safe landings.

Orville and Wilbur did not only study gliders. They also studied birds. They tried to copy the way birds used their wings. They made an aircraft with bendable wings.

Their first successful flight was before Christmas in 1903. Their plane was called the *Wright Flyer*. It was different from a glider. It had a motor. The first flight lasted twelve seconds. Orville flew 120 feet.

The brothers made three more flights that day. Wilbur flew for fifty-nine seconds. He went 852 feet.

At first, not many believed the Wright brothers. How had they created a new way of flying? So many others had failed before them.

In the beginning, the brothers did not want to tell how they had built their plane. They feared that someone would steal their design. But soon, Orville showed others the plane. The brothers did a show in France in 1908.

Orville and Wilbur made better and better planes. They formed the Wright Company. It designed, built, and sold airplanes.

Planes today are much safer than the earliest ones. However, air travel would not even exist without the hard work of Orville and Wilbur Wright.

King and the Bus Boycott

Martin Luther King, Jr., was born in Atlanta, Georgia, in 1929. During this time, black people and white people were segregated, or kept apart. Schools and other public places, like restaurants, had sections for black people and sections for white people. This was the law. Young Martin felt this law was wrong. He wanted everyone to be treated the same.

Martin loved to learn, and he was a good student. He went to college 3 years early, when he was only 15 years old. In college, King learned about Mahatma Gandhi. He was a peaceful man who helped the people of India. They were treated poorly by India's leaders. Indian people suffered injustice, just as black Americans did. But instead of fighting and yelling, Gandhi used words and actions. Dr. King wanted to follow the nonviolent methods used by Gandhi. Maybe these methods would help black Americans.

Dr. King giving a speech

King and the Bus Boycott, continued

In 1955, Dr. King found a way to use these nonviolent methods. It started when a black woman named Rosa Parks was riding a bus.

In Montgomery, Alabama, the buses were segregated. That meant she was supposed to give up her seat to a white person. One day, she refused to do that. She was arrested.

Dr. King leading a march

King was upset about Mrs. Parks' arrest. Dr. King led marches and organized a bus boycott. He asked black people to stop riding the buses. The boycott was supposed to last only one day, but it went on for 381 days! All this time, thousands of black people walked instead of taking the bus. The bus companies lost money. Many people tried to stop the boycott. But King and his followers would not back down.

The year-long boycott was successful. The law was changed. Buses were integrated, and black people started riding again. But this time, they sat wherever they wanted.

Informative Text

Hedgehogs

A hedgehog is a small wild animal. Hedgehogs grow to be as little as 4 inches or as long as 12 inches. They have faces shaped like cones and sharp spines over most of their bodies. The sharp spines stay on the hedgehog for over a year before they fall out. Then new spines grow. The spines help the hedgehog protect itself from other animals that want to eat it. Owls and foxes are some animals that eat hedgehogs. When a hedgehog feels scared, it rolls itself into a ball so only the spines show.

Hedgehogs live in Europe, Asia, Africa, and New Zealand. They can live in many different habitats. A hedgehog can live in a forest, in a desert, or even in a person's garden. A hedgehog digs a big hole in the ground and builds a nest to sleep in. A hedgehog's nest can be made of leaves, tree branches, and grass.

A hedgehog sleeps most of the day and comes out at night to eat frogs, bugs, worms, mice, roots, and fruit. The hedgehog can't see very well, but it can smell and hear well.

Farm Art

As you drive through Salinas, California, you will see lettuce, lettuce, and more lettuce. That's because Salinas grows most of the country's salad greens. Look out the window, and you pass one field after another. Lots of workers are in the fields, bending over, cutting lettuce. Others are packing the lettuce in boxes. They all look so busy. Wait! Did you see that? Are those giant people in that field?

Yes, they are giant people. They are 18 feet tall! The figures are in the middle of a farm. They show real people who once worked there. The farm owner wanted to show the community that it takes a lot of people to grow food. We see lettuce piled up neatly at the grocery store. But we hardly think of all the people who get the lettuce from the farm to our table.

The workers are an important part of the farm and of the community. That's why the farm owner asked John Cerney, a local artist, to find a way to honor the workers.

Farm Art, continued

Farmers and business people love Cerney's work. His workshop is a busy place. Cerney starts with an idea. He takes many photos of the person who is the model. He studies the photos and finds the perfect one. Then he draws the person on small, thin pieces of plywood.

He doesn't see the whole piece of art until later. He puts the pieces together outside, like a giant puzzle. When it's all put together, he stands back and looks up at his work. Up close, you can see the puzzle pieces. But when you're zooming by in a car, you see a huge person that you didn't expect to see.

Since the artwork is done on thin sheets of plywood, the sun, wind, and rain wear down the wood. So the figures may only last six or seven years. Cerney already has had to redo several of his giant people. "They won't last forever. Only in books and pictures, but that's okay," says Cerney.

Locals and tourists enjoy the giant outdoor art. It is part of the landscape.

This giant cut-out is 40 feet long. It is made of 550 plywood pieces that Cerney painted. Then he put them together like a puzzle.

I Need a Dog

written by Summer York
illustrated by D. Kent Kerr

Dear Mom and Dad,

I am writing you a letter.

I need a pet dog.

I want a black and white border collie.

They are very smart dogs.

I will teach him commands.

He will sit and stay.

I will feed him.

I will walk him every day.

I will keep him clean.

He will not get fleas.

I will be very responsible.

I will play with him in the backyard.

He will be my best friend!

All I want for my birthday is a dog.

I will not ask for any other gifts.

I am begging you.

I need a dog!

Thanking Veterans

Veterans Day is a national holiday that happens every year on November 11. It is a special holiday in the United States to honor veterans. Veterans are men and women who have served in the military.

The United States military is made up of five different groups. There are the U.S. Army and the U.S. Navy. There are the U.S. Marine Corps and the U.S. Air Force. The U.S. Coast Guard is also part of the military. We honor all of the people who have worked in these groups on Veterans Day.

Veterans Day is a holiday across the whole country. Many businesses are closed that day. Many people don't have to go to work or school. Post offices are closed and no mail is delivered. Some places have big military parades. Other places have large parties to thank their veterans. You can celebrate, too. If you see someone in the military on Veterans Day, say, "Thank you for your service!" That person worked hard to keep us safe and free.

People clap and cheer for veterans during Veterans Day parades. Veterans often carry flags that stand for their groups. They also carry the flag of the United States.

You Should Exercise

written by Summer York
illustrated by Brian Cibelli

Everyone should exercise.
Exercise keeps you healthy.
There are many ways to exercise.
All exercise is helpful.

Exercise helps your body.
It makes your muscles strong.
It builds up your bones.
It keeps you at a healthy weight.
It can even help you sleep.
You should take care of your body.
Exercise is a good way to do this.

Exercise helps your mind.
It can make you feel happy.
It gives you confidence.
It gives you skills.
Your mind is a very powerful tool.
You should think about caring for it.
Exercise can keep your mind healthy.

Exercise can be fun.
Play a team sport.
Ride your bike up and down the street.
Walk your dog.
Swim with friends.
Try something new.
Exercise does not need to feel like work.
You should enjoy it!

Exercise is good for you.
You should exercise every day.

Baby Blue Whale

The largest baby animal in the world is the baby blue whale. A blue whale calf can weigh up to three tons when it is born. Whales are mammals. Like all mammals, the blue whale calf drinks its mother's milk. The milk is very rich in fat. In its first year, the baby blue whale grows 200 pounds a day. Wow!

When it is born, the mother blue whale pushes her calf to the ocean's surface for its first breath. Just like its mother, it needs to breathe air. Then every few minutes, it swims to the surface to breathe. At the surface, the calf breathes out. It blows misty air out through two blowholes on top of its head. The mist sprays high into the air! Then the calf takes in more air through its blowholes.

The whale calf starts to eat food when it is about six months old. Just like its mother, it eats tiny shrimp-like animals called krill. Blue whales have layers of baleen instead of teeth. Baleen is made of the same stuff as fingernails. It is like a big comb. The whale takes a huge gulp of ocean water. The baleen lets the water out, but not the krill.

Adult blue whales can be up to 100 feet long. That is about as long as three school buses! Adult blue whales are the largest animals in the world.

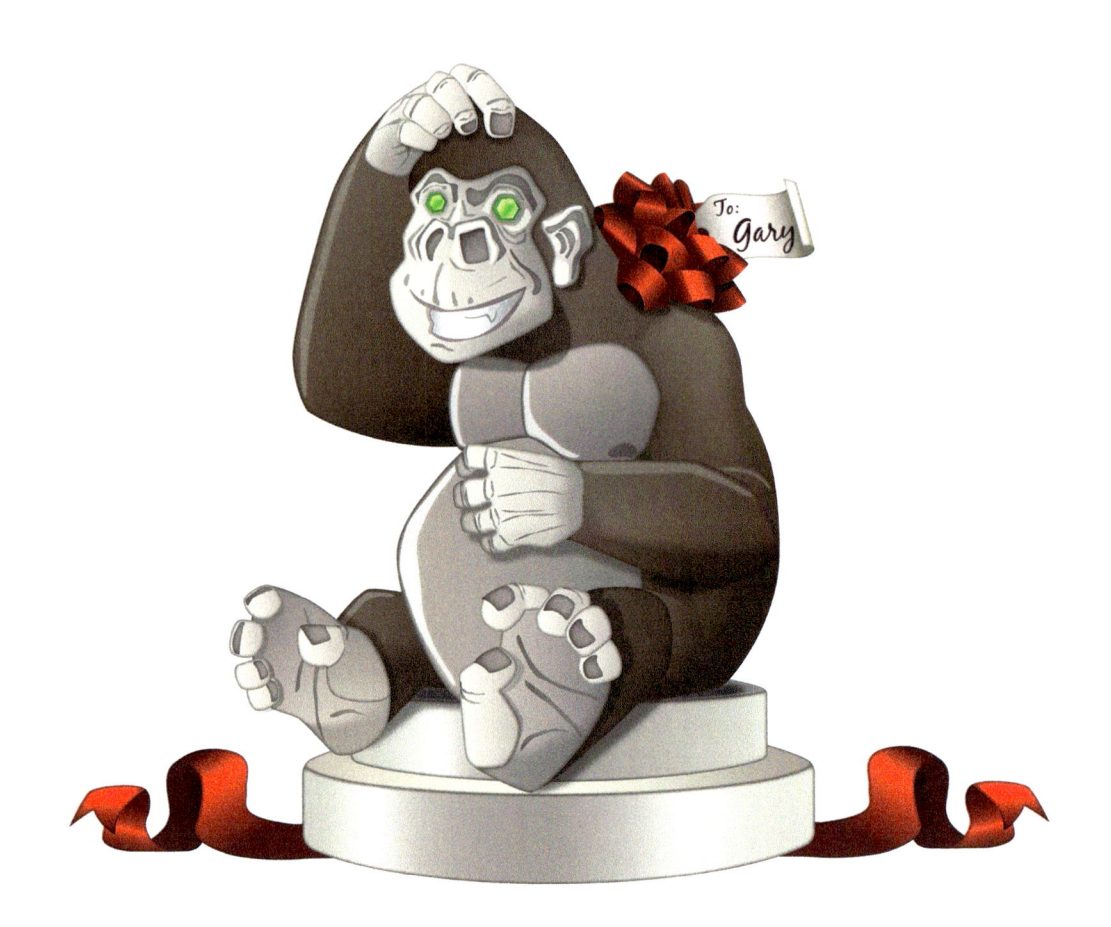

Gary's Gift

written by Summer York
illustrated by D. Kent Kerr

My uncle Gary sure is strange.

He owns a gym at the edge of town.

He puts grape jelly on his eggs.

Gross!

Gary's granny, Gert, wanted to give him a generous gift.

Yesterday he got the gigantic box.

Gary gasped when he opened it.

Next, he grinned a glad grin.

The gift was a giant gorilla statue.

It was four feet tall!

It had glittering green gems for eyes.

Gary was giddy over his gorgeous gorilla.

Gary named it George.

He proudly put George outside his gym.

Then a strong gust of wind blew George over.

The gorilla broke on the ground.

Its green gem eyes got lost in the hedges.

I guess I was glad.

The guests were gawking at it too much.

Gary had to throw George in the garbage.

Now he is sad about his strange gift.

A Day with Dicky

written by Vincent J. Scotto
illustrated by Sean Ricciardi

Now listen to the tale of Dicky the dog. Dicky was a fast dog. He loved to run. His owner, Kevin, could not keep up. Dicky ran everywhere he went. Kevin would chase him, but Dicky was too fast. Dicky always found his way back to Kevin. One day, Dicky ran too far and got lost.

Kevin and Dicky went to the dog park one day. The park was surrounded by a fence. Kevin thought it was safe to let Dicky off his leash. Dicky ran straight for the fence as fast as he could. He jumped so high that he made it over the top. Daring Dicky dashed downhill away from Kevin. Dicky was soon into the willowy woods at the bottom of the hill. Dicky became scared when he lost his way. He ran back and forth looking for the way out.

It started to get cold. Dicky thought he would never find his way out. Dicky stopped running around. He lay in some leaves to stay warm. Dicky felt hopeless. He missed his warm bed in his house. He missed Kevin holding his hairy head at night. Suddenly, Dicky heard a familiar sound.

Dicky heard Kevin's voice. Kevin was calling him from a distance. Dicky darted toward his friend. Dicky saw Kevin at the edge of the woods. Dicky pounced perfectly into Kevin's arms. The two were so excited to see each other. Dicky licked Kevin's face with love. Kevin laughed and scooped Dicky up. Kevin and Dicky headed home happily.

Dicky never ran away from Kevin after that. Dicky still ran fast. Now he only ran where he could still see Kevin. Dicky learned his lesson: Running fast may be fun, but running too far can be dangerous.

Flip, Flop, Thump

written by Michael Scotto
illustrated by Evette Gabriel

Flip, flop, flip, flop. Harmony Wannadogood pranced along. "Oh, how I love the springtime!" she said.

It was a warm, sunny day in Midlandia. Harmony skipped through Playland Park in her new spring sandals. They were as green as the grass. They had a yellow flower on each strap. Sandals were Harmony's favorite kind of shoe. She liked the sound they made as she walked: *flip, flop, flip, flop.*

Harmony stopped to look at the leafy trees. Suddenly, a red, round blur whizzed past her face. "Yikes!" she said. The red thing bounced into a tree trunk nearby.

"Careful!" a voice called out. It was Coach. He ran toward her.

"What was that?" asked Harmony.

"*That* was a home run!" said Coach.

Coach bent down and picked up the red object. He showed it to Harmony. "It's a kickball!" Harmony realized. "Are you playing a game right now?"

Coach nodded. He pointed to the field behind them. Harmony saw Midlandians in T-shirts playing. Sparky was running around the bases. Everyone was having a great time.

"I've never played kickball before," said Harmony.

"Do you want to join us?" asked Coach.

Harmony's face lit up. "Yeah!" she cried. "Let's go!" She started to jog toward the game: *flip, flop, flip, flop—*

"Hold it!" barked Coach. "You can't play in those sandals. They are not good for running. Plus, you'd hurt your toes when you kicked the ball!"

"Oh," Harmony said, disappointed.

"However," Coach said, "I have an extra pair of sneakers in my gym bag. You can wear them."

Harmony grinned and followed Coach back to the playing field. Coach went behind home plate to his bag. He pulled out a pair of sneakers. "Try these on," he said.

Harmony put the sneakers on. They fit perfectly! "I'm ready to go!" she declared.

She ran to the outfield, listening to the sneakers. They did not make a cool sound like *flip, flop, flip, flop.* They just went *thump, thump, thump.* "The sound isn't as nice," Harmony thought, *"but they are better for running."*

Then, all of a sudden, Harmony tripped. She tumbled into the grass. Harmony was stunned! "What in the world did I trip over?" she wondered.

Harmony stood up, went to her spot, and waited.

After a minute, Harmony's friend Dewey kicked the ball deep into the outfield. "I'll catch it!" Harmony called out. She ran at top speed toward the falling kickball: *thump, thump, thump*….

Crash! Harmony tripped again! The ball bounced to the ground beside her. "What is wrong with these shoes?" she wondered.

Soon, Harmony's team traded sides. It was their turn to kick. Harmony stepped up to home plate. She was excited to take a turn! She wanted to make a great kick and run the bases.

Harmony backed up to make her kick. Sparky rolled the kickball toward her. Harmony hurried forward to kick: *thump, thump, thump*—

Splat! Harmony flipped head over heels and flopped into the dirt. "That is it!" Harmony yelled. "I can't do this!"

"Time out!" yelled Coach. He came over to speak with Harmony. "What's wrong?" he asked.

"These sneakers are broken!" she replied. "Every time I try to run in them, I flip and flop about! It's like some invisible thing keeps tripping me!"

Coach looked at Harmony's sneakers. "Aha!" he said. "I see your problem! You didn't tie your shoelaces!"

"Shoelaces?" asked Harmony.

"You know, these strings at the top of your shoes!" Coach said.

"I'm supposed to tie those?" asked Harmony. "I thought they were just a decoration."

Coach chuckled. "It's important to tie your shoes," he said. "As you found out, it can be unsafe to run around with loose laces. Luckily, there are quite a few ways to tie them tight. If you'd like, I can teach you my favorite way to tie a shoe."

"That would be super!" said Harmony.

Coach smiled. "I'll show you how to tie one shoe," he said, "and then you tie the other."

Coach started to tie, describing each step. "First," he explained, "you need to take your two laces and make a knot. Then, you take each lace and make it into a loop."

"Those look like bunny ears!" Harmony said.

"That's right!" Coach said. "You take the two bunny ears and cross them like an *X*. Loop one ear under the other and pull it tight. That, my dear friend, is one way you can tie a shoe. Knot, loop, cross, loop, pull. You try!"

Harmony got to work on her other shoe. She spoke as she tied. "Knot…loop…cross…loop…pull!" she said. "I did it!"

"Knot, loop, cross, loop, pull," Coach agreed. "Now you're really ready to play. Give her another shot, Sparky!"

Harmony backed up again to kick. Sparky rolled her the ball. Harmony ran forward: *thump, thump, thump*….

Bam! Harmony kicked the ball all the way into the outfield. She ran around the bases—*thump, thump, thump*—until she was safe at home plate.

"Home run!" shouted Coach.

Everyone on Harmony's team cheered. Harmony shook Coach's hand. "Thanks for helping me, Coach," she said. "I love to flip and flop, but only when I'm wearing my sandals."

Limerick Collection

1

There was a young lady whose bonnet
Came untied when the birds sat upon it.
But she said, "I don't care!
All the birds of the air
Are welcome to sit on my bonnet!"

2

There was an old person whose habits
Induced him to feed upon rabbits.
When he'd eaten eighteen
He turned perfectly green
Upon which he relinquished those habits.

3

There was a young lady whose eyes
Were unique as to color and size.
When she opened them wide
People all turned aside
And started away in surprise.

—Edward Lear

Sampan

Waves lap lap
Fish fins clap clap
Brown sails flap flap
Chopsticks tap tap
Up and down the long green river
Ohe Ohe lanterns quiver
Willow branches brush the river
Ohe Ohe lanterns quiver
Waves lap lap
Fish fins clap clap
Brown sails flap flap
Chopsticks tap tap

—*Tao Lang Pee*
translation by Channing and Olive Wence

A Wildflower Surprise

written by Sarah Marino

Near the end of May, Tracy and her mother decide to grow a wildflower garden. It will bloom in the summer. "Today is a nice, sunny day," Tracy's mother says. "Let's plant the seeds today!"

Tracy watches her mother gather the seeds in a bowl. Tracy does not understand why the seeds are so tiny. "Mama, are you sure these little things turn into flowers?" she asks. "They are so small, and they are green and brown. How will they make purple flowers?"

"I know they are tiny," her mother says, "but this is what plants look like before they grow into flowers. These are seeds. We will put them into the earth. There, they can sprout and make flowers."

Tracy and her mother take the seeds to the backyard. Tracy's mother has made a special place where they will plant the garden. Tracy uses a little shovel and helps her mother. She digs two narrow rows about ten feet long. They place the seeds into the rows.

Then Tracy's mother covers them with soil. Tracy uses the watering can to give them a drink.

"When will the seeds turn to flowers, Mama?" Tracy asks.

"Not for many weeks," her mother answers. "We will see them come out of the ground bit by bit. Someday, they might be as tall as you!"

Every day Tracy goes to the garden to see if the seeds have grown. For several weeks, nothing happens. But then, one day after a rainstorm, she finds something new. Little green shoots have risen out of the dark soil. They are just a few inches high, but Tracy is so excited! She crawls on her belly to get a closer look at them.

"Mama, look," Tracy says, pointing to the shoots. "The seeds turned into little plants!"

"Yes, they did!" her mother says. "Just a few more weeks, and they'll turn into flowers!"

The plants seem to grow very slowly after that. Soon, it is July. By then they are only as tall as Tracy's knee. None of them have flowers.

One day when her granddad is visiting, Tracy shows him the garden. "Granddad, these are supposed to be flowers, but they're not," she says.

"They will grow flowers soon," Granddad tells her. "It takes longer than one month. You must be patient. They need lots of sunlight and water to grow."

"But when will they be pretty and have purple and pink flowers?" Tracy asks.

Granddad bends down to inspect a plant. Then he pulls Tracy into a hug. "It will happen soon, my little dove. Just wait and see."

By August, Tracy has almost forgotten about the flowers. On a very hot Saturday morning, she finds her mother sitting outside near the garden. She sees an orange butterfly float above her mother's head. The butterfly flutters down and lands on… could it be? Yes, it's a purple flower!

"Mama, there's a flower and a butterfly!" Tracy says, running close to see.

"Yes, there are lots of flowers. Aren't they pretty?" her mother asks.

"Yes!" Tracy looks around. Some flowers are almost as tall as she is. There are so many colors! Some flowers are purple, some are pink, some are blue, and others are yellow and orange.

A yellow butterfly lands on a blue flower. Then a honey bee flies to a white flower nearby.

"Can you smell the flowers?" her mother asks.

Tracy sniffs the air. "They smell good, and they're so colorful!"

"I know it took time," her mother says, "but remember those tiny seeds we planted? Those seeds have become these flowers. It was worth waiting for, right?"

"Yes, it was!" Tracy says.

They sit in the grass and watch the flowers, butterflies, and bees. Tracy has a feeling that August might be the best month of the summer!

Neighborhoods: Where Will You Live?

written by Vincent J. Scotto
illustrated by Sean Ricciardi

Where will you live when you grow up? Have you ever thought about that? It depends on what kind of life you want to live. There are many kinds of places to live. There are three main types of neighborhoods. Which one will you choose?

One type of neighborhood is called an urban neighborhood. These are found in cities and large towns. Urban neighborhoods are very lively. Many people live very close together. There are lots of tall buildings. Stores and housing can be close together. People move at a quick pace throughout the day. There are not many trees or animals. Most of an urban neighborhood's space is filled up by people. Would you like to live in an urban neighborhood?

Suburban neighborhoods are another type of place to live. A suburb is mostly made up of housing. Homes are separate from stores and businesses. Malls and shopping centers are found in suburbs. Suburbs are usually located just outside of cities. They are close enough for one to take a short drive to get to the city. Some people live in suburbs and work in the city. Would you like to live in a suburban neighborhood?

Rural neighborhoods are quite different from other kinds. There are not many people at all in a rural neighborhood. Most rural areas have farms and forests. Many animals live in rural neighborhoods. Houses are spread far apart. Most houses have lots of land for one family. It can be a long distance to the next town or to a city. Many people love that part the most. They like to stop and take it slow. Urban life is too fast for them. Would you like to live in a rural neighborhood?

There are many types of neighborhoods. There are good things about each one. It all depends on what a person likes. Do you like busy streets with lots of people? Do you like shopping malls? Do you like lots of land with trees? Think about these questions. They will help you decide what neighborhood to live in when you grow up.

Force and Motion at Play

written by Debbie Parrish

Did you ever ride a roller coaster
Or push some bread down in a toaster?
Did you ever take a wagon ride
Or get pushed on a swing outside?

If you did, then you should know
That push and pull make all things go.
Let's talk now about the very notion
That you can have fun with force and motion!

The roller coaster pulls you to the very top
So you can push down to a thrilling stop.
You push the bread all the way down,
Then pull it out when it turns toasty brown.

When a friend pushes your swing just right,
You feel like you're soaring right out of sight!
The force of push or pull, it's true,
Causes the movement a thing can do.

Blowing wind will push your kite,
Until you pull the string back tight.
Then the kite moves back toward you
Until the wind's force pulls it out of view!

What does the force set out to prove?
Only that a thing will have to move.
Up, down, around, or through—
And many more ways than that few!

'Twas the Morning of Earth Day

written by Jill Fisher

'Twas the morning of Earth Day and
all through the yard,
No litter could be found, not even a card.

A rainbow was hung in the blue sky with care,
In hopes that great Mother Nature would come there.

The animals stirred from their nests and their beds,
Where visions of flower buds had
bloomed in their heads.

On that day in late April, the sun shined so bright.
Everyone worked to make Earth a sweet sight.

Green trees were planted and the parks were all cleaned.
It was the prettiest thing the animals had seen.

Then to everyone's joy came a guest they all liked:
Mother Nature herself! She rode a pink bike.

She helped to sort plastic, paper, and glass.
Each went in its own box. She moved really fast!

Soon Earth Day was done and it was time for bed.
Mother Nature was so pleased that she said,

"Reduce, reuse, and recycle, no matter who you are!"
Then off she flew, with a trail of white stars.

I Asked My Mother

I asked my mother for fifty cents

To see the elephant jump the fence.

He jumped so high that he touched the sky

And never came back till the Fourth of July.

—Anonymous

Way Down South

Way down South where bananas grow,

A grasshopper stepped on an elephant's toe.

The elephant said, with tears in its eyes,

"Pick on somebody your own size."

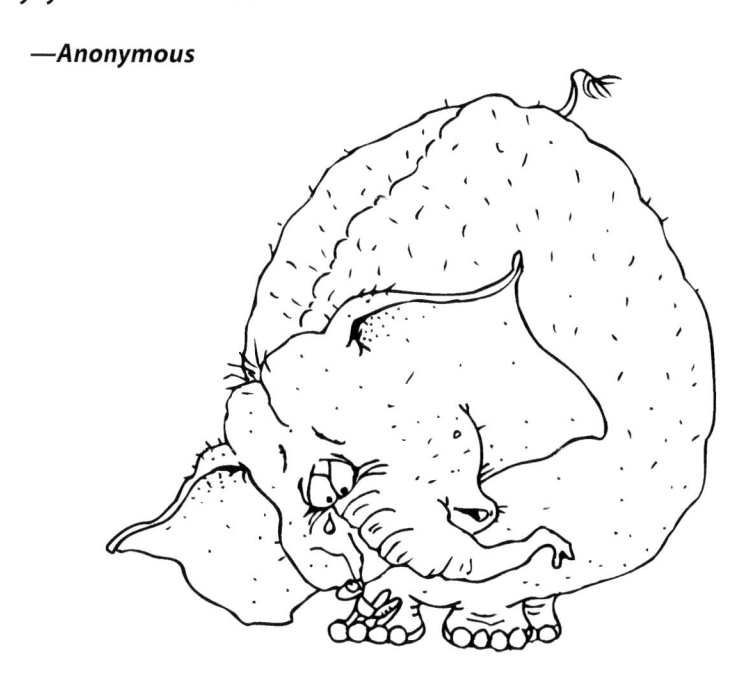

—Anonymous

April's Trick

There's a bug on your back,
And it's yellow and green.
You've spots on your face
I'll bet you've not seen.
There's a rip in your coat,
And your hair's turning gray.
Don't get upset though,
It's April Fools' Day.

—*Martin Shaw*

Ladybug, Ladybug

Ladybug, Ladybug
Stay right here.
Don't fly home,
You have nothing to fear.

Your children are sleeping.
Your husband is shopping.
Your father is sweeping.
Your mother is mopping.

Your grandma is strumming.
Your grandpa is clapping.
Your auntie is humming.
Your uncle is napping.

Your brother is riding.
Your sister is cooking.
Your niece is hiding.
Your nephew is looking.

Ladybug, Ladybug
Stay right here.
Don't fly home,
You have nothing to fear.

—John Himmelman

Fly Away, Fly Away

Fly away, fly away over the sea,
Sun-loving swallow, for summer is done;
Come again, come again, come back to me,
Bringing the summer, and bringing the sun.

—*Christina Rossetti*

Pumpkins

Pumpkins oval, pumpkins round,
Pumpkins tumbling on the ground;
Pumpkins giant, pumpkins small,
Pumpkins lined against the wall;
Pumpkins squat and pumpkins high,
Pumpkins piled to the sky.
Pumpkins orange, pumpkins gold;
Pumpkins even white, I'm told.
Pumpkins fat and pumpkins thin,
Pumpkins with rough, bumpy skin.
Pumpkins pretty, pumpkins fun;
Oh, how can I pick just one?

—*Virginia Kroll*

I Had a Little Pig

I had a little pig,
I fed him in a trough,
He got so fat
His tail dropped off.
So I got me a hammer,
And I got me a nail,
And I made my little pig
A brand-new tail.

—*Anonymous*

Silly Things

Shoes have tongues
But cannot talk.
Chairs have legs
But cannot walk.
Needles have eyes
But cannot see.
This chair has arms—
But it can't hug me!

—*Anonymous*

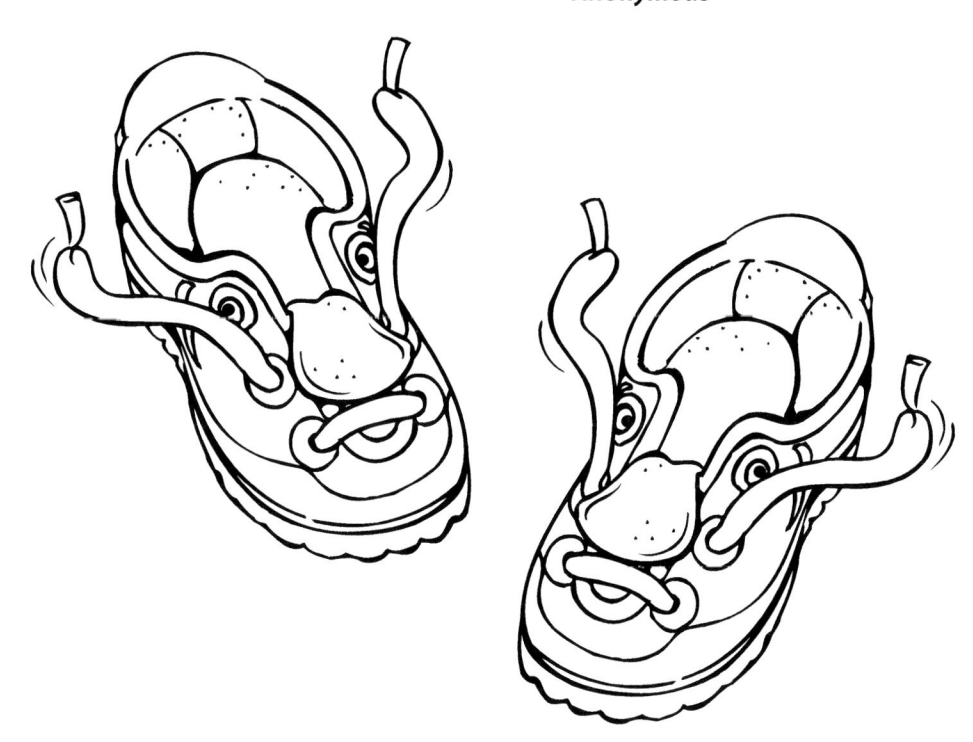

Teddy Bear, Teddy Bear

Teddy bear, teddy bear,
    Turn around.
Teddy bear, teddy bear,
    Touch the ground.

Teddy bear, teddy bear,
    Show your shoe.
Teddy bear, teddy bear,
    That will do.

Teddy bear, teddy bear,
    Go upstairs.
Teddy bear, teddy bear,
    Say your prayers.

Teddy bear, teddy bear,
    Turn out the light.
Teddy bear, teddy bear,
    Say good night.

—*Anonymous*

The Squirrel

Whisky, frisky,
Hippity hop,
Up he goes
To the treetop!

Whirly, twirly,
Round and round,
Down he scampers
To the ground.

Furly, curly,
What a tail!
Tall as a feather
Broad as a sail!

Where's his supper?
In the shell,
Snappity, crackity,
Out it fell.

—*Anonymous*

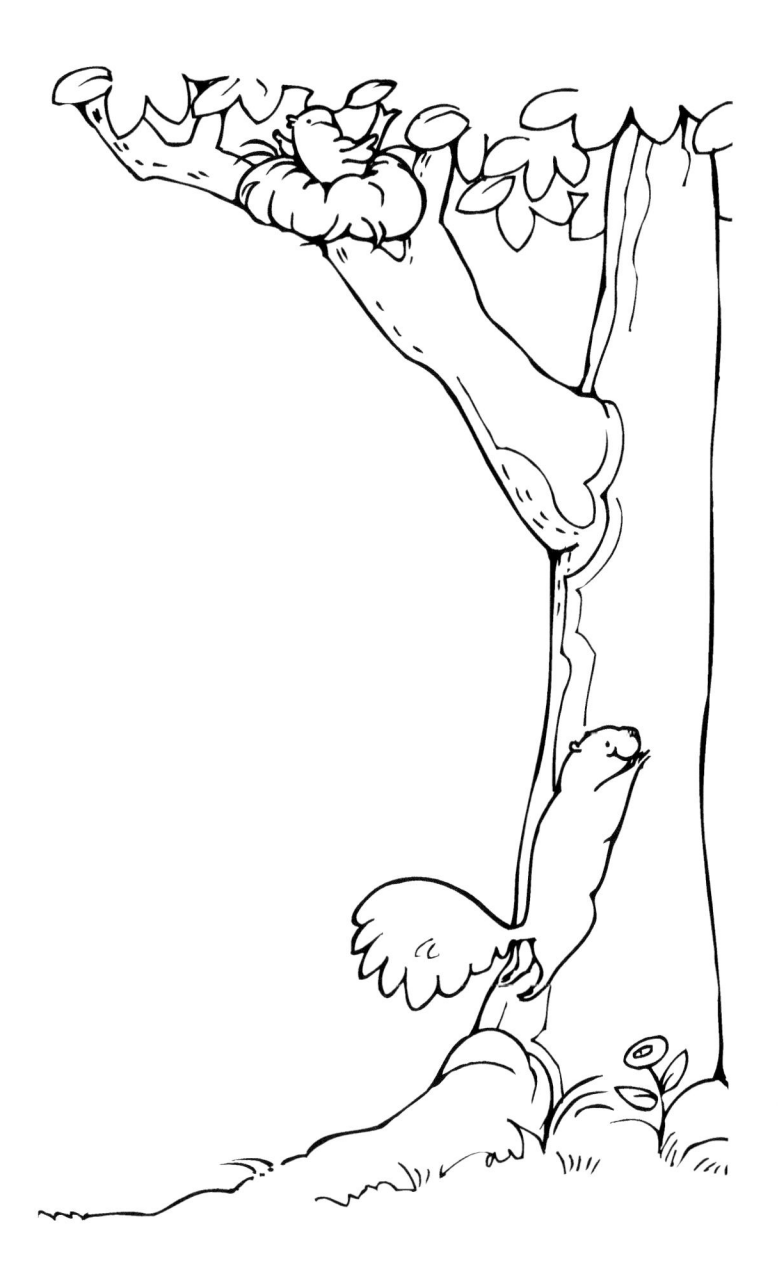

Late for School!

written by Summer York
illustrated by Brian Cibelli

I sat up. I rubbed my eyes. What time was it? I stared at the clock. It read 7:45 a.m. Oh, no! I flew out of bed. I was late!

The school bus always came at eight o'clock. I needed to hurry. I panicked. My heart raced. Why didn't Mom wake me up?

I threw open my closet doors. I dug through piles of clothes. I tugged on a shirt. My new shoes were missing! I had to wear my old ones.

Next, I raced into the bathroom. No time to shower! I pulled the comb through my hair. I splashed my face. I quickly brushed my teeth.

Then I rushed downstairs. I raced into the kitchen. There was no breakfast on the table. I glanced around. I stumbled through the darkness. Where was everyone?

"Mom? Dad?" I called. No answer. I searched for something to eat. I rattled through cabinets. It would be a miracle if I caught the bus.

"Let's go!" I demanded. Silence. I ran from room to room. I was confused. I sprinted up the stairs. I smacked right into my mom. She stared at me.

"It's Saturday," she said. She laughed. I rolled my eyes. I felt foolish.

I headed back to bed.

The Snake

Slick and silent,
near my toe,
through the leaves,
I see it go.
Over sticks
I watch it glide,
looking for a place to hide.
Slow and sliding,
does it know,
I'm scared of how it
slithers so?
Sly and sleek,
it slips away.
I'm glad it passed me by
today!

—Janet Lawler

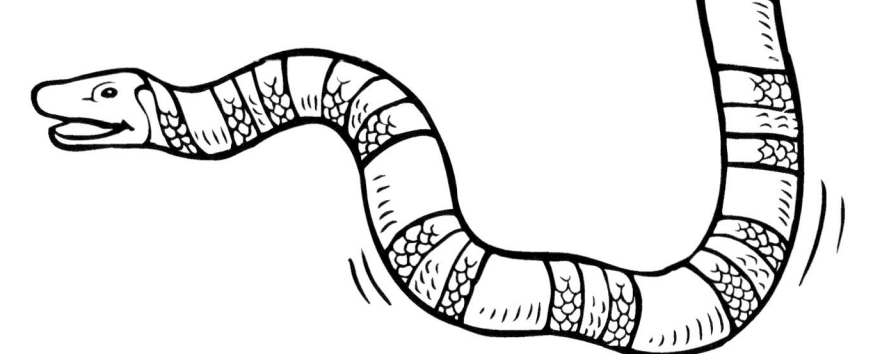

My Perfect Weekend

written by Jennifer Tkocs
illustrated by Mallory Senich

This weekend, I went on an adventure! It was with my best friend, Emma. Her family has a cabin at Lake Erie. They invited me to come along.

I had never been to Lake Erie before. I didn't think it would be that great. There are lakes near my house. Those lakes are not very special. But Lake Erie was great!

Lake Erie is enormous! We drove up in a van. The cabin is two miles from the lake. It is very nice. Emma and I had our own room. It was just like we were sisters for the weekend!

Soon, it was time to hit the beach. I did not know Lake Erie had beaches. It has many of them! We put on our swimsuits. Emma's mom drove us to a beach.

Emma and I made sandcastles all day. We had a contest to see who could make the biggest sandcastle. Emma won. I think she had more practice!

Emma's dad packed us a picnic lunch. He made the best sandwiches! They had mayonnaise, salami, and ham. He even put on big lettuce leaves from Emma's mom's garden.

During lunch, we noticed two puppies with the family next to us. "Let's call them over!" said Emma.

We called to the puppies and they came to our towel. "Look, Molly!" Emma said. "That one loves you!"

"She just loves my lunch," I said. The puppy tried to take a bite of my sandwich.

Emma and I stayed at the beach all day. We read comic books under our umbrella. We drank juice boxes. We listened to the radio.

At sunset, Emma's parents took us to dinner. We went to a restaurant that is in an old firehouse. They made the tastiest fries! And we got to look at the old fire equipment. We saw pictures of the firefighters from the early 1900s.

When we got back from dinner, the weather had changed. It was chilly and breezy since the sun had gone down. "I have the perfect solution for this cool, summer night," said Emma's dad.

Emma's mom took out the board game Clue. It is my and Emma's favorite. "You girls get this set up," she said. Emma's mom made us hot chocolate. Her dad made a fire in the fireplace.

We sat in front of the fire. We played three rounds of Clue. We drank our hot chocolate. We laughed and talked about our day. At bedtime, Emma and I were so tired. We fell right to sleep.

The next morning, we loaded up the car and headed back to Pittsburgh. This was a great weekend. Any time Emma asks me to go with her to Lake Erie, I will say yes!

July

Crunch, munch,
Have some lunch!
Family picnic in the park.

Whizzle, fizzle,
Sparklers sizzle.
Write your name into the dark.

Tooting, hooting,
Flag saluting,
Big parade goes marching by!

Booming, zooming,
Colors blooming.
Fireworks light up the sky.

—*Lana Krumwiede*

Hush, Little Baby

Hush, little baby, don't say a word.
Mama's gonna buy you a mockingbird.
If that mockingbird won't sing,
Mama's gonna buy you a diamond ring.
If that diamond ring turns brass,
Mama's gonna buy you a looking glass.
If that looking glass gets broke,
Mama's gonna buy you a billy goat.
If that billy goat won't pull,
Mama's gonna buy you a cart and bull.
If that cart and bull turn over,
Mama's gonna buy you a dog named Rover.
If that dog named Rover won't bark,
Mama's gonna buy you a horse and cart.
If that horse and cart break down,
You'll still be the sweetest little baby in town.

—Traditional

The New-England Boy's Song about
Thanksgiving Day

1 Over the river, and through the wood,
To grandfather's house we go;
The horse knows the way,
To carry the sleigh,
Through the white and drifted snow.

2 Over the river, and through the wood,
To grandfather's house away!
We would not stop
For doll or top,
For 'tis Thanksgiving Day.

3 Over the river, and through the wood,
Oh, how the wind does blow!
It stings the toes,
And bites the nose,
As over the ground we go.

4 Over the river, and through the wood,
With a clear blue winter sky,
The dogs do bark,
And children hark,
As we go jingling by.

5 Over the river, and through the wood,
To have a first-rate play—
Hear the bells ring
Ting a ling ding,
Hurra for Thanksgiving Day!

6 Over the river, and through the wood—
No matter for winds that blow;
Or if we get
The sleigh upset,
Into a bank of snow.

7 Over the river, and through the wood,
       To see little John and Ann;
          We will kiss them all,
          And play snow-ball,
       And stay as long as we can.

8 Over the river, and through the wood,
       Trot fast, my dapple grey!
         Spring over the ground,
         Like a hunting hound,
       For 'tis Thanksgiving Day!

9 Over the river, and through the wood,
   And straight through the barn-yard gate;
         We seem to go
         Extremely slow,
       It is so hard to wait.

10 Over the river, and through the wood,
       Old Jowler hears our bells;
         He shakes his pow,
         with a loud bow-wow,
       and thus the news he tells.

11 Over the river, and through the wood—
     When grandmother sees us come,
        She will say, Oh dear,
        The children are here,
      Bring a pie for every one.

12 Over the river, and through the wood—
      Now grandmother's cap I spy!
        Hurra for the fun!
        Is the pudding done?
      Hurra for the pumpkin pie!

              —*Lydia Maria Child*

The Swing

How do you like to go up in a swing,
Up in the air so blue?
Oh, I do think it the pleasantest thing
Ever a child can do!

Up in the air and over the wall,
Till I can see so wide,
River and trees and cattle and all
Over the countryside—

Till I look down on the garden green,
Down on the roof so brown—
Up in the air I go flying again,
Up in the air and down!

—Robert Louis Stevenson

The Pasture

I'm going out to clean the pasture spring;
I'll only stop to rake the leaves away
(And wait to watch the water clear, I may):
I sha'n't be gone long.—You come too.

I'm going out to fetch the little calf
That's standing by the mother. It's so young,
It totters when she licks it with her tongue.
I sha'n't be gone long.—You come too.

—Robert Frost

Navajo Chief's Blankets

There are many different ways that people make art. Weaving is one kind of art. People who weave put thread together to make cloth. Weavers can make blankets. They can make clothes. People can weave beautiful and useful things.

The Navajo people are Native Americans. The Navajo have been weavers for hundreds of years. Navajo weavers make beautiful designs, or patterns. Today's Navajo weavers still use designs from long ago. Some of the designs have changed. Some have stayed the same. Let's look at how one design has changed.

One type of Navajo blanket is called a chief's blanket. There are three kinds of these blankets. That is because the designs changed over time. Each kind has its own name.

A first-phase chief's blanket has simple stripes.

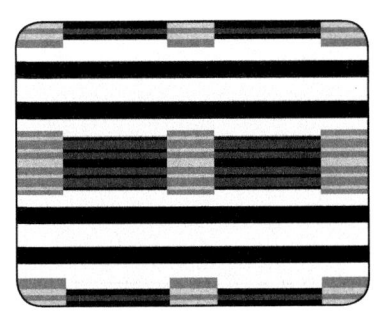

A second-phase chief's blanket has stripes. It also has rectangles.

A third-phase chief's blanket has stripes, diamonds, and half-diamonds. Sometimes, the diamonds have more patterns inside of them.

Owl Facts

Owls are large, interesting birds. In some ways, all owls are alike. All owls have large heads. They have circles of feathers around each of their eyes. Owls can't move their eyes like we can. They have to move their whole head to look around! All owls have sharp claws on their feet. The claws help them catch food and sit on tree limbs.

In some ways, owls are different from each other. Snowy owls and barn owls have features and habits that make them different from each other.

Snowy owls are white. They have more feathers on their legs than other owls. Their feet have extra padding for walking on snow. Snowy owls make low hooting sounds. Most of these large owls live in the Arctic. The Arctic land is very flat. Snowy owls make their nests right on the ground. They hunt for food during the day and the night.

Snowy Owl

Barn owls have white faces that look like hearts. Their bodies are small, but their wings are large. Barn owls are usually light gray with some spots. Barn owls do not hoot. Instead, they make a hissing or screeching sound. Barn owls hunt for food only at night. They live all over the world. They make their nests in tree holes, buildings, or barns.

Barn Owl

Colossal Crazy Horse

South Dakota is famous for Mount Rushmore, the huge carving of four presidents. Nearby, there's another mountain carving. This one will be even bigger than Mount Rushmore. It's colossal! When it is finished, it will be the largest sculpture in the world. It's called the Crazy Horse Memorial.

Memorials honor important people. The Crazy Horse Memorial is a way to honor Native Americans, especially the Lakota people. They lived in the area that is now South Dakota. The Lakota people had a chief named Crazy Horse. He was a kind leader. They wanted a monument to remember him by.

They invited an artist named Korczak Ziolkowski to make the monument. First he made a sketch of the chief on horseback, with his arm pointing. Ziolkowski began carving the mountain in 1948.

Colossal Crazy Horse, continued

This is what the Crazy Horse Memorial looked like in 2012.

He used special tools to chip away at the rock. He worked alone for many years. He died in 1982, before he could finish the face of the chief. Ziolkowski's wife and seven of his children continued carving. They are still chipping away at the mountain today. The horse's head will be next. It will be huge. All four of the Mount Rushmore faces would fit inside this horse's head!

When will the monument be finished? No one knows for sure. Until then, the Ziolkowski family will continue to chip away.

This painting shows what the memorial will look like when it is finished.

What Will a Magnet Attract?

How do the papers on this refrigerator stick to the door? They aren't glued on. Magnets hold the papers there. Magnets also keep refrigerator doors shut.

Magnets come in many shapes and sizes. Here are just a few:

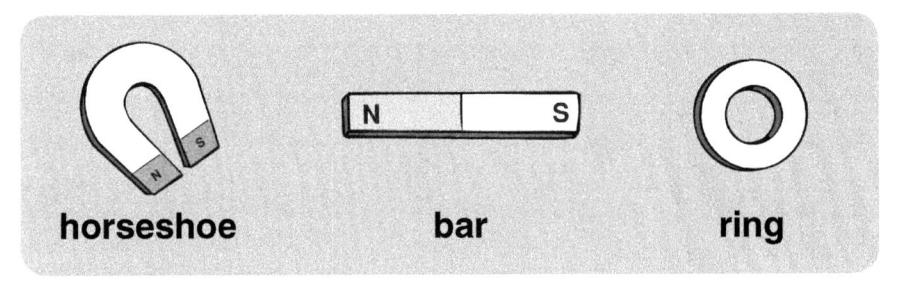

horseshoe   **bar**   **ring**

Magnets stick to objects made from some kinds of metals. Magnets use a force called magnetism to attract these metals. An object that attracts metal is called magnetic. A magnetic object will not attract things like glass or wood.

A magnet will not stick to all things made of metal. A magnet will not stick to coins. They do not have iron in them. Magnets only attract metals with iron in them. Steel is a metal with iron in it.

A magnet will attract some things made of steel. Many refrigerators are made of magnetic steel. So are things like paper clips, pins, nails, and cars.

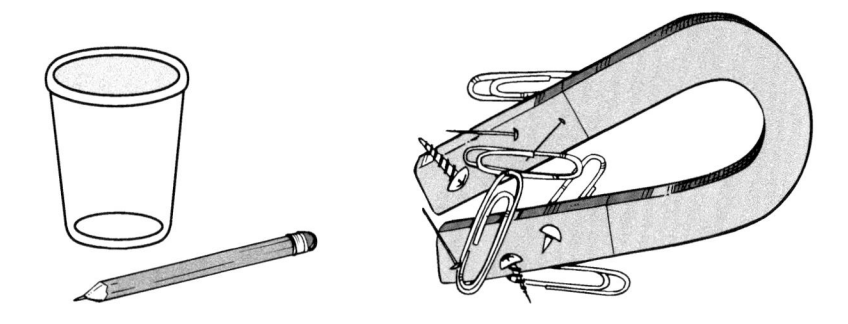

Most magnets will attract a metal object even if something thin is between the object and the magnet. Hang a picture on the refrigerator, and a magnet will hold it in place. But a refrigerator magnet won't hold up a book. The magnet isn't strong enough.

A refrigerator is just one magnetic object. Look around. Find something that a magnet might attract. It shouldn't be too hard to find. Magnetism is all around!

A Strong Leader

The United States has a president. The president is the leader of the nation. The president's job is one part of the government. The government is made up of all the people who help run our country. The president is chosen by the people every four years. People in the United States vote for the president they want. If you are 18 years old, you can vote. You can help choose the next leader of the United States.

President Barack Obama was United States president from 2009 to 2017.

The president of the United States is a very important person. However, even the president must follow the laws of the Constitution. The Constitution tells about the powers and duties of the president. It gives the president the power to sign new laws. The president is also in charge of the armed forces.

The president meets with leaders from other countries. They talk about world problems. They try to work together to make the world a better place for everyone. Being the president of the United States is a hard job. But the president is able to help many people with his or her work.

The president flies in an airplane called Air Force One. He or she can fly to other countries to work with their leaders.

Coquís and Other Frogs

There are many different kinds of frogs in the world—4,740 different kinds, to be exact! Frogs can be found all over the world, except in Antarctica. Most frogs live in places that have warm weather.

When most people think of frogs, they think of big frogs that are green. But there are blue, yellow, red, orange, and spotted frogs as well. The most beautiful frogs are blue. Some frogs are big and some are small. Some live in trees, and others live on the ground.

a bullfrog

a tiny coquí on a stem

Of all the frogs in the world, I like the coquí frog the best. A coquí is a tree frog. Coquís are very tiny, only an inch long. They live on the island of Puerto Rico, which is in the Caribbean. A coquí sings a song every night. It sounds like this: "Ko-Kee!" The coquí's song is the most beautiful sound in the world.

Coquís are different from most frogs. Most frogs have webbed feet. But coquís have special toe pads on their feet that help them climb on leaves and trees. Coquís are the best frogs.

Leopard Sharks

Leopard sharks are small sharks. Unlike some other sharks, leopard sharks are scared of humans. They will swim away quickly if they see you.

Shapes and Sizes

Leopard sharks are long and slim. They are named after leopards because they have dark spots on their bodies like leopards do. Leopard sharks have short round snouts. They can grow to be 6 feet long and weigh up to 40 pounds.

What They Eat

The foods leopard sharks eat usually live on the bottom of the ocean. Leopard sharks are known to eat crabs, shrimp, small fish, and fish eggs. Their mouths are curved near the bottom of their heads. This makes it easy for the sharks to swim near the bottom of the ocean and suck up their tasty treats.

a leopard shark swimming at the Monterey Bay Aquarium

Where They Live

Leopard sharks live in cool or warm water. You can find most leopard sharks down the Pacific coast of North America, from Oregon to Mexico. They do not like to stay in deep oceans but prefer to swim near sandy flats, kelp reefs, and rocky areas.

Run, Bird, Run!

Faster than a rattlesnake! Quicker than a lizard! It's a bird. It's a plane. It's a…roadrunner!

This speedy bird can run up to 15 miles per hour. It can fly if it wants to, but running is more useful. The roadrunner can even jump straight up to catch a meal. It eats bugs and desert animals like snakes and mice.

Most birds are afraid of humans. But the roadrunner is not scared of people. It might walk right up to get a close look at someone. Then off it goes again!

Giant Pandas

What is black and white and bleats like a sheep? A giant panda! There are very few giant pandas in the world. In the wild, they live in bamboo forests. These forests are found only in parts of China. Some giant pandas are in zoos around the world. These pandas were gifts from China.

Giant pandas can eat bamboo for 12 or more hours a day. That's a lot of bamboo! They have paws with a toe that works like a thumb to grab the bamboo. They have big strong teeth for chewing bamboo.

Giant pandas are born alive. The babies are very small when they are born. These tiny babies are pink with no hair. Their eyes are closed. As they grow, the young pandas get black spots on their skin. Panda mothers feed and protect their babies for many months.

China wants to protect the giant pandas living in the bamboo forests. Land has been set aside where giant pandas can live safe from harm. Someday there may be many more pandas in the world.

The Golden Fish
A Russian Folktale

In a land far away lived a poor old man and his wife. They lived in an old shack with a crooked roof. The old shack was on a small hill near the sea. Their only food was the fish that the old man caught.

Each morning the old man took his fishing net down to the sea. He would throw the net into the cool, blue water. Then he would pull it back in filled with fish. One day, when he pulled the net back in, he saw something shiny. It was a golden fish. The golden fish began to speak. It begged the old man to throw it back into the water. "If you let me live, I will grant you a wish."

The kind old man didn't ask for anything. He just put the golden fish back into the water. When he got home, the old man told his wife what had happened. She was very angry. "Go back and ask the fish for a loaf of bread for us to eat!" she shouted.

The old man did as his wife asked. He caught the golden fish again. "Please may I have a loaf of bread," he asked the fish. When he got home, a loaf of bread was on the table.

© Evan-Moor Corp. EMC 757

The old man's wife said, "The fish gave us one wish. Maybe he will give us more." The next day, she told her husband to ask the fish for a new washtub. He did as his wife asked. When he got home, there was a new washtub in the front yard. But his wife was not happy.

Each day she wanted more. She wanted a new house. She wanted to be rich. She wanted to be queen. Each time the golden fish granted her wish.

But even being queen did not make the old woman happy. She sent her husband to the golden fish one last time. She wanted to rule the land and sea and everything that lived there. The old man caught the golden fish and made the wish.

"Go home," said the golden fish. "Your wife will get what she should have."

When the old man got home, he saw his wife dressed in rags. She was standing inside the old shack. And there was not even a loaf of bread left to eat.

The Goose That Laid Golden Eggs
An Aesop Fable

A farmer and his wife went to a fair in the next town. They wanted to buy a new goose to eat the weeds in their garden. They found a large, plump goose and took her home. They didn't know that this was their lucky day.

The next morning, the farmer's wife went to collect eggs. She found a big yellow egg in the goose's nest. She picked up the strange egg and took it to her husband. "Look at this egg the goose laid," she said. "It is very heavy and very yellow."

The farmer took the egg. His mouth fell open. "This egg is made of gold," he said.

The goose laid a golden egg every day. The farmer and his wife grew very rich from selling the eggs. And they grew very, very greedy.

"Let's cut open the goose. Then we can get all of the golden eggs at one time," said the farmer. But when they cut the goose open, there was no gold. The goose was just like all geese inside. Now the greedy farmer and his wife had no more golden eggs. And they didn't have a goose to eat the weeds in the garden.

The farmer and his wife kept buying geese. They wanted to find a new goose that laid golden eggs. But they were out of luck.

A Bell for the Cat

The cat was causing a terrible problem. It was catching and eating all of the mice! "What can we do? What can we do?" cried the mice.

One of the older mice called a meeting. "We need to find a way to solve this problem," said the mouse. "How can we keep that hungry cat from catching any more of us?"

The mice talked and talked and talked. No one could think of a good way to solve the problem. At last, a little mouse stood up. He said, "I know what to do. The cat can sneak up on us because it is so quiet. We should put a bell around the cat's neck. Then we could hear when it is coming and run for cover."

"Hoorah!" shouted the other mice. "We're saved! We're saved! We'll put a bell on the cat!"

As the mice shouted with joy, a quiet old mouse stood up. The old mouse said, "I think a bell on the cat is a good plan. It would give us a chance to escape that hungry cat. But, tell me, just who will put it there?"

The room became very quiet. Slowly each mouse left the room. No one wanted to bell the cat.

The Pancake

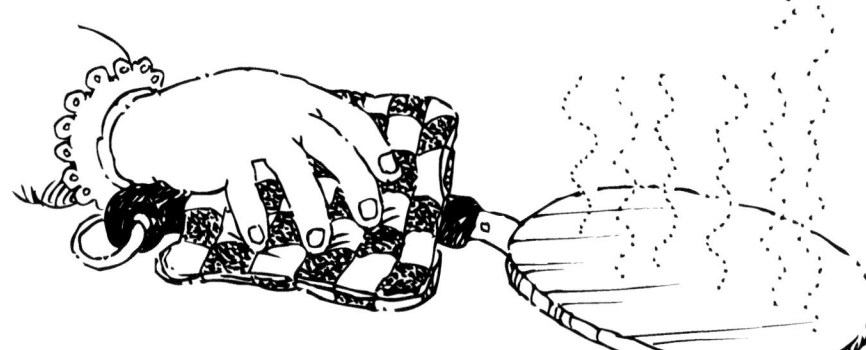

Long ago and far away there was a farm wife. She had seven hungry children. One morning she said, "I think I'll cook a large, tasty pancake for breakfast." Her children smelled the pancake cooking and came to beg for a bite.

"Give me a bite of pancake, Mother. I am so hungry," said her first child.

"Dear Mother," said the second.

"Dear, sweet Mother," said the third.

"Dear, sweet, nice Mother," said the fourth.

"Dear, sweet, nice, pretty Mother," said the fifth.

"Dear, sweet, nice, pretty, good Mother," said the sixth.

"Dear, sweet, nice, pretty, good, kind Mother," said the seventh.

"I will give you a bite when the pancake is done," said their mother.

All at once, the pancake jumped off the griddle. It rolled through the door and down the hill.

"Stop, pancake!" shouted the farm wife. She ran after the pancake with the griddle still in her hand. Her seven hungry children followed as fast as they could go.

"Stop, pancake!" they all screamed. But the pancake rolled on and on until they couldn't see it.

The pancake rolled on until it met a hen. "Good day, Pancake," said the hen. "Don't roll so fast. Rest awhile and let me eat you."

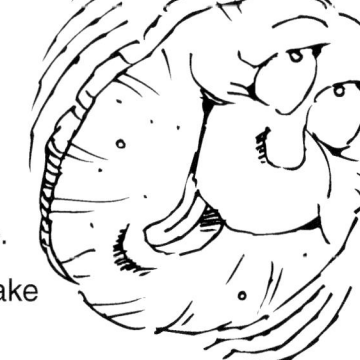

"I ran away from the farm wife and her seven hungry children," said the pancake. "I will run away from you, too, Henny Penny." And the pancake rolled on. Soon it met a duck.

"Good day, Pancake," said the duck. "Don't roll so fast. Stop a little and let me eat you."

"I ran away from the farm wife and her seven hungry children and from Henny Penny," said the pancake. "I will run away from you, too, Ducky Lucky." And the pancake rolled on. Soon it met a pig.

"Good day, Pancake," said the pig.

"The same to you, Piggy Wiggy," said the pancake.

"Don't be in such a hurry," said the pig. "Let's travel together to the other side of the forest. It's not safe in there."

So they went along together. Soon they came to a brook. Piggy Wiggy swam across the brook. But the poor pancake couldn't get over. "Sit on my snout and I'll carry you over," said the pig.

The pancake did not stop to think. It just hopped up onto Piggy Wiggy's snout. As quick as a wink the clever pig swallowed the pancake. That is the end of the pancake. And that is the end of our story.

The Tortoise and the Eagle
An African Fable

Eagle spent his time in the clouds. Tortoise spent his time on the ground. So the two didn't meet often.

One day Eagle went to visit Tortoise. Frog had told him that Tortoise was kind to his guests. Eagle wanted to see if this was true. It was! Tortoise asked Eagle to come in and fed him a tasty meal.

The food was so good that Eagle came back again and again. Every visit he ate all of Tortoise's food. But Eagle never invited Tortoise to his home.

One day Frog heard Eagle talking to himself. Eagle said, "Ha! I've eaten Tortoise's food many times. But he can't reach my home to eat mine."

Frog thought, "Tortoise is my friend. I will go tell him what Eagle is doing."

So Frog went to Tortoise's house. He said, "Eagle is laughing about never having to feed you. He knows you can't reach his home in the treetop. But I have a plan. Here's what you can do." And he told Tortoise the plan.

The next day Eagle came again. Tortoise said, "Please let me give you a gourd full of food. It is a gift for your wife."

While Eagle ate his meal, Tortoise went into the kitchen. He climbed into a large gourd and his wife piled food on top of him so he couldn't be seen. She gave the gourd to Eagle.

When Eagle reached home, he put the gourd on the floor. He was surprised to see Tortoise roll out of it. "I have come to visit you," said Tortoise. "When do we eat?"

The selfish Eagle became angry. He said, "You'll be the only meal here!" He tried to peck Tortoise's hard shell. He didn't hurt Tortoise. He just hurt his own beak.

"I can see you are not my friend after all," said Tortoise. "Take me home." And he grabbed Eagle's leg.

Eagle flew up into the sky and tried to shake Tortoise off. "I'll throw you to the ground. You'll smash into little bits!" he cried.

But brave Tortoise kept his hold on Eagle's leg. At last Eagle gave up. Eagle took Tortoise home and let him go.

As Tortoise walked into his house he looked back at Eagle. He said, "Friends share with each other. You have been selfish and unkind. Don't come back again."

The Fox and the Stork
An Aesop Fable

Long ago Fox and Stork were friends. One evening Fox invited Stork over for dinner. As a joke, he served only a shallow dish of thin soup. Fox lapped up the soup, but Stork could get only a few drops with her long, narrow bill.

"I am sorry that you do not like the soup," said Fox as he laughed behind Stork's back.

Stork did not complain or say that Fox was unfair. She just said, "Will you come to my house for dinner soon?" Fox quickly agreed to dine with Stork the following evening.

When Fox arrived at Stork's house, he smelled a delicious aroma. "I wonder what tasty meal Stork has cooked?"

Fox hurried to the table. Stork had made a stew filled with tiny bits of meat and vegetables. Stork brought the stew to the table in a tall jar with a narrow mouth. Now it was Stork's turn to laugh. She reached into the jar with her long, narrow bill and ate the delicious stew. Poor Fox sat by and watched. He could not get his snout far enough into the jar to reach the stew. He could only lick off the bits left on the mouth of the jar.

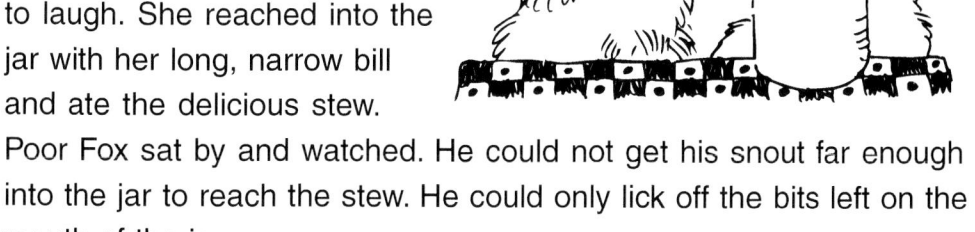

After dinner the hungry fox headed home. He knew that he could not blame Stork. He had been unkind to her. Fox had learned that you should treat others the way you want to be treated.

The Rabbit That Ran Away

A Fable from India

A nervous rabbit sat under a palm tree. A coconut fell to the ground behind her. When she heard the noise, she jumped up. "The Earth is breaking apart!" she thought. Without even looking to see what had made the noise, she started to run as fast as she could.

Another rabbit saw her running. He called out, "Why are you running, Miss Rabbit?"

"I don't have time to stop," said the rabbit. "The Earth is breaking apart, and I am running away!"

When the other rabbit heard this, he began to run, too. Each rabbit they met ran with them after hearing that the Earth was breaking apart. Soon hundreds of rabbits were running as fast as they could.

Then larger animals like deer and tigers began to join them. Each animal cried, "The Earth is breaking apart!" and ran as fast as it could.

A wise old lion saw the animals running and shouting. He ran in front of them and roared, "STOP!"

This stopped the animals. They knew they must obey the King of Beasts. "How do you know the Earth is breaking apart?" asked the lion.

The little rabbit stepped forward and said, "Oh, great king, I heard it."

"Where did you hear it?" asked the lion.

"I was resting under a palm tree. Then I heard the sound of the Earth breaking apart," said the little rabbit.

"Come and show me where this happened," said the lion.

"No, no," said the little rabbit, "I can't go near that tree. I'm too frightened."

"I will carry you on my back," said the lion. So the little rabbit went with the lion back to the palm tree. There they saw the big coconut lying under the tree.

"You silly rabbit," said the lion. "It was the sound of the coconut falling on the ground that you heard. The Earth is not breaking apart." The lion scolded the rabbit. "Be sure that what you are saying is true before you tell others."

Then the lion ran back and told the other animals what had really happened. The animals walked away whispering, "The Earth is not breaking apart."

If it hadn't been for the wise old lion, the animals might still be running.

The Little People

A Native American Fable

Long ago, when my people lived close to nature, little people lived on the Earth. Even though they were small, they were very powerful.

This story tells what happened when my great-great-great-grandfather met two of the little people.

One day, when he was just seven, a little boy went hunting. He took his bow and arrows to shoot small birds. It was the way growing boys learned to hunt. It was their schooltime.

The little boy walked along the river, looking for water birds to shoot. Suddenly, he heard a sound on the water. He was surprised to see a tiny canoe coming down the river. In the canoe were four of the tiniest little men he had ever seen. They rowed the canoe right up to the boy and stopped.

The little men greeted the boy. Then one of the men asked, "Would you like to trade your bow and arrows with one of us?"

The boy didn't stop to think. He just said, "No, thank you. It would be silly to trade. Your bow and arrows are much smaller than mine."

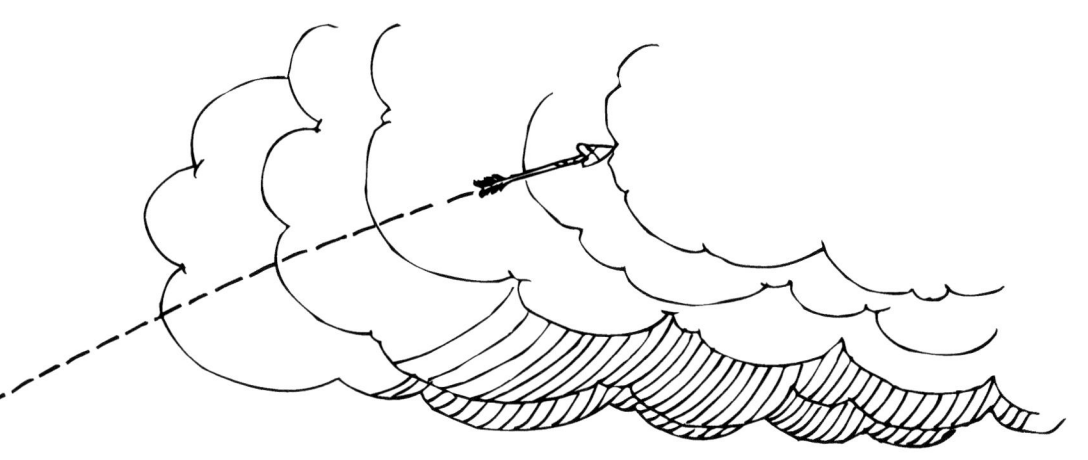

One of the tiny men took his bow and shot an arrow straight up. The arrow disappeared into the sky. The boy watched and waited, but the arrow did not come back down. The little man said, "Remember what I say, small one. The biggest things are not always the best."

The little men stepped back into their canoe. They picked up their canoe paddles and set off down the river. They soon disappeared around a bend in the river.

The boy ran home moving as swiftly as a young deer. "Come quickly!" he shouted. "I have something to tell you."

His family gathered around to hear his tale. His parents frowned as he told the family what had happened. His grandfather scolded the boy. He said, "You made a big mistake not trading with the little people. One of their bows and arrows would have made you a mighty hunter. Bigger is not always better, my grandson."

That day my great-great-great-grandfather learned a lesson. It is a mistake to judge people by their size. You never know who or what they may really be.

This lesson has been handed down from father to son in my family ever since.

The Frog Prince
A Folktale from Germany

The king gave his youngest daughter a golden ball. It was her favorite toy. One day, as she was playing, the golden ball fell into a deep well. The princess sat by the well weeping. She heard someone say, "What is the matter, little one?" She looked up and saw a large, ugly frog.

"My golden ball has fallen down the well. I can't reach it," sobbed the princess.

"If you take me home and let me be your best friend, I will get the ball," said the frog.

"Oh, yes!" promised the princess. But as soon as the frog handed her the golden ball, she ran back to the castle.

"Wait for me!" shouted the frog as he hopped after her.

The princess ran into the castle and shut the door. She wanted to forget her promise to the frog.

That night at dinner, there was a knock at the door. It was the frog. The king asked the frog, "Why have you come to the castle?"

The frog told the king what the princess had promised him in return for his help. "Well," said the king, "she must do as she promised."

The frog hopped up next to the princess. He began to eat off her plate. When the princess started to complain, her father frowned and told her to be quiet.

After dinner the king told his daughter to take the frog to bed with her. She knew she had to obey her father. She did what he said, but she was not happy about it. The frog fell asleep on a pillow next to the princess.

When she woke up the next day, the first thing the princess saw was the frog. She cried out, "You slimy thing. Get off my bed!" and threw the frog against the wall.

Right before her eyes, the frog changed into a young prince. "Thank you for saving me," he said. "I was under a spell. I had to remain a frog until a princess kept her promise to me."

The king was happy that his daughter had learned to keep her promises. The prince was happy that he wasn't a frog. And the princess was happy that she no longer had to eat and sleep with a frog.

The Monkey and the Crocodile
A Folktale from India

A family of monkeys lived in a tree by a riverbank. A family of crocodiles lived in the river. The mother crocodile watched the monkeys for a long time. One day she said to her son, "My son, catch one of those monkeys for me. I want to eat its heart."

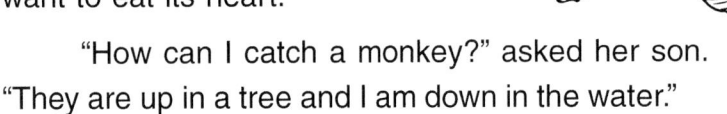

"How can I catch a monkey?" asked her son. "They are up in a tree and I am down in the water."

"You're a smart crocodile. I'm sure you can think of a plan," answered his mother.

The crocodile thought and thought. At last he had a plan. In the center of the river was an island. On the island were trees filled with ripe fruit. He would trick a monkey into coming down for some of the fruit.

"Little monkey," called the crocodile, "the fruit on the island trees is ripe now. Would you like some to eat?"

The monkey liked ripe fruit, but he couldn't swim. "How can I get across to the fruit?" asked the monkey.

"Hop on my back and I'll carry you across," said the crocodile.

The monkey was hungry, and wanted some of the fruit, so he jumped onto the crocodile's back.

Halfway across the river, the crocodile dove under the water. When he came back to the surface, the monkey gasped for air. "Why did you take me under the water, crocodile?" he asked.

"My mother wants to eat a monkey heart," answered the crocodile. "I am going to drown you and take her your heart."

Thinking quickly the monkey said, "I wish you had told me you wanted my heart. I left it back home in my tree. If you want my heart, we must go back to get it."

"Very well," said the crocodile. "I'll take you back so you can get your heart and bring it to me. Then we'll go to the island."

Well, as soon as the crocodile came near land, the monkey jumped off his back. He climbed up into the high tree branches. "My heart is up here. If you want it, you will have to come up to get it," he called down to the crocodile.

The crocodile had to return home and tell his mother that he couldn't get a monkey heart. The monkey and his family soon moved to a new tree far away from the crocodiles.

The Tiger and the Big Wind
A Folktale from Africa

Long, long ago there was a time when the rains had not come for a whole year. Without much food and water, all of the animals had become very hungry and very thirsty.

In all the hot, dry land there was one place where underground water had kept a large fruit tree alive. The juicy fruit was just waiting to be eaten. Why didn't the animals eat the fruit, you ask? A large tiger was resting under the tree.

Tiger was mean and selfish. He sat in the shade of the tree all day growling whenever any other animal came near. Tiger would say, "Stay away from my tree or I'll eat you up!"

One day a rabbit heard the animals of the forest talking about what was happening. "Oh, Wise Rabbit, what are we to do?" the animals asked.

Wise Rabbit thought about this for several days. Finally he called the animals together and said, "Listen and I will tell you what to do."

Early the next morning, while Tiger was still sleeping, the animals hid in the forest near the field where the fruit tree grew. The animals that lived on the ground stood near big, hollow logs. The animals that lived in the trees sat in the branches. The animals waited patiently for Wise Rabbit to arrive.

When Rabbit came, he was carrying a large rope. Rabbit ran across the field shouting, "Oh, my! Oh, my!"

The noise woke Tiger and he growled, "Stop making that horrible noise, Rabbit. I am sleeping!"

© Evan-Moor Corp. • EMC 757

"Run, Tiger, run! A big wind is coming. It will blow everyone off the Earth!" As Rabbit said this, all the animals hiding in the forest began to make a loud racket.

The birds began to flap their wings, causing the leaves in the trees to shake about. The large animals began to beat on the hollow logs, making a terrible racket. Other animals ran around in the brush, until the whole forest seemed to be swaying in a terrible wind.

Tiger was terrified! "What should I do?" he screamed.

"You must run and try to find a safe place," said Wise Rabbit. "I can't help you now. I have to tie down the small animals with this rope or they will be blown off the Earth."

"You must tie me down first!" demanded Tiger.

Wise Rabbit shook his head, "You are strong enough to take care of yourself. I must help the smaller animals."

Tiger roared. "You must tie me up now or I will eat you!"

"Very well," said Wise Rabbit. "I will tie you up first." He tied Tiger tightly to the tree. When he was done, the rabbit called for the other animals to come out of the forest.

"Look at this greedy tiger," said Wise Rabbit. "He wanted to keep all of the fruit for himself instead of sharing with us. He forgot that food was put on the Earth for all to enjoy."

The selfish tiger could only watch as the animals sat together in the shade of the tree and feasted on the delicious fruit.

The Four Musicians
A German Folktale

An old donkey had grown weak and unable to work. When he learned that his owner was going to do away with him, the donkey ran away. "I will go to the city and become a musician," thought the donkey.

Along the way he met an old hound dog, a toothless old cat, and a rooster. They all had the same story to tell. They were too old to work and their owners were going to kill them. So each of the animals had run away. "Come with me to the city," said the donkey. "You can become musicians, too."

The four new friends walked along until it began to grow dark. The rooster flew to the top of a tree. He looked around to find some place for them to spend the night. "I see a light in an old building not far from here," said the rooster. "Let's see if we can stay there."

When they reached the building, the donkey peeked through a window. Inside were a gang of robbers sitting around a table covered with good things to eat. The gold they had stolen was scattered around the table, too.

"If we chase them away, we will have food and shelter," said the donkey. Very quietly, the donkey put his front feet on the window ledge. The other animals jumped up onto his back. The four friends started to sing. The donkey brayed, the hound dog howled, the cat screeched, and the rooster crowed.

The noise was so horrible that the robbers nearly knocked each other over in their haste to run away.

The four friends ate the food that the robbers had left behind. Then they settled down for a good night's sleep. The donkey lay down on some straw in the front yard. The hound dog lay down by the front door. The cat lay down in front of the fireplace. And the rooster perched on a beam of the roof. Soon they were fast asleep.

After midnight the leader of the robbers sent a man to check out the house. If it was safe, they would go back to get their gold.

When the man peeked in, he didn't see the animals in the dark. Feeling braver, he went in the front door. He saw the old cat's eyes shining in the darkness. Thinking it was a monster, he ran screaming from the house. As he ran out of the house, he stepped on the dog, who bit him in the leg. As he ran across the yard, the donkey kicked him in the back. The man's screams woke up the rooster, who started to crow.

When the man got back to the forest, he told the robbers how horrible it had been. "A monster with eyes of fire lives in that building. Another monster stabbed me in my leg with a knife. Then a big black monster beat me with a wooden club. A little monster on the roof kept calling, 'Chuck him up to me!' I didn't think I was going to get away!"

The robbers agreed that no amount of gold was worth going back into that horrible place. The four friends were so happy and comfortable that they never went to the city. And they never became musicians.

The Shoemaker and the Elves
A German Folktale

Once upon a time there was a kindly shoemaker. Times were hard and he couldn't earn enough money to live on. All he had left was the leather for one pair of shoes. The shoemaker cut out the shoes and set them aside. He planned to sew them later.

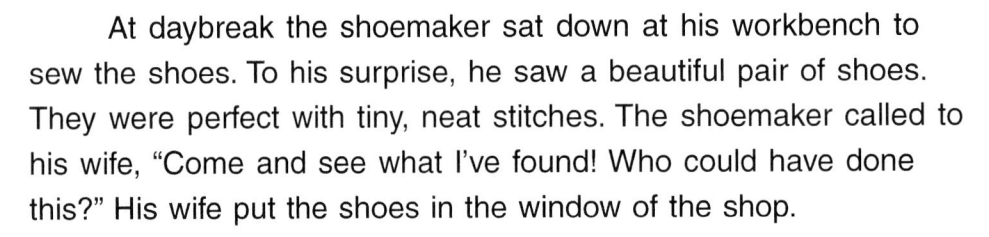

At daybreak the shoemaker sat down at his workbench to sew the shoes. To his surprise, he saw a beautiful pair of shoes. They were perfect with tiny, neat stitches. The shoemaker called to his wife, "Come and see what I've found! Who could have done this?" His wife put the shoes in the window of the shop.

Soon a customer came into the shop. "How much are those beautiful shoes in the window?" asked the woman. "I must have them for my husband."

With the money from the sale of the shoes, the shoemaker bought leather to make two more pairs. Again the shoemaker cut out the shoes and left them on his workbench to finish the next day.

In the morning the shoemaker found that both pairs of shoes had been finished. His wife put the shoes in the shop's window. Soon both pairs of shoes had been sold for a high price. Before long the shoemaker and his wife were making a good living.

© Evan-Moor Corp. • EMC 757

One evening the shoemaker said to his wife, "I'm going to wait up tonight to see who has been doing my work for me." His wife agreed to wait with him. That night the couple hid behind a curtain to see what would happen.

As the clock struck midnight, two tiny elves, barefooted and dressed in rags, appeared. The elves hopped up onto the workbench and quickly went to work. They sewed and tapped and polished shoes until daybreak. Then the elves left as quickly as they had come.

"Oh, my!" exclaimed the shoemaker's wife. "I have never seen such a sight in all my life. Those hard-working elves have made us rich. What can we do to thank them?"

"I will make them shoes," decided the shoemaker. "You can make them something to wear."

The shoemaker made each elf a pair of tiny shoes. His wife made each elf a shirt, a coat, and a pair of trousers. When the clothes were finished, the shoemaker laid them on the workbench. He and his wife hid behind the curtain to see what the little elves would do.

At midnight the elves hopped up onto the workbench as they did every night. When they saw the clothes lying there, the elves began to laugh. They dressed themselves in the twinkling of an eye. The elves danced out the door and down the street and were never seen again.

Paper Airplane

written by Luke See

Gathering Materials:

To make a great paper airplane, you need a good sheet of paper. Try finding a sturdy piece of printer paper or copier paper. Cardstock and other thicker kinds of paper might be too heavy to fly. Grab a few extra pieces for practice. The only other material you need is tape. Double-sided tape is best, but regular tape is fine as well. Now that you have your materials, it is time to start folding.

Creating the Airplane:

1. First, turn the paper sideways, or horizontally. From there, make a vertical fold straight down the middle. Now unfold the paper. The piece of paper should look like an open book.

2. Next, take the bottom-right corner of the page and fold it up and inside. The fold should line up with the center line you created. Repeat this step with the bottom-left corner of the page.

3. After that, take the diagonal edge you created and fold the entire thing into the center line. Do this for both sides of the paper. This fold should feel similar to the previous step. Once you have completed this step, you should have a shape that is starting to resemble an airplane.

4. Next, you need to create the wings of your airplane. Take the right side of the plane and fold it out and down. In other words, instead of folding in toward the center line, fold the edge of the plane down onto itself. Match the top edge of paper with the bottom edge of the plane's body. Repeat this step for the left side/wing.

5. The shape of your plane should now be complete. At this point, you should be able to pinch the plane from the bottom and hold it by its central fold. The last thing you need to do is stick a piece of double-sided tape on the inside of the plane's body. Try placing the tape toward the front of the paper airplane, near where the cockpit might be. If you do not have double-sided tape, try folding a piece of tape onto itself to make a small, sticky square. The tape will help your plane retain its shape.

6. You are now ready to fly your airplane. Find an open place where you can try a few test flights.

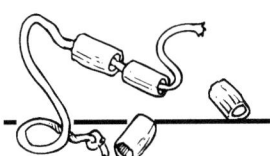

Make a Necklace

Read how to do it carefully. Follow steps: 1, 2, and 3. . . .

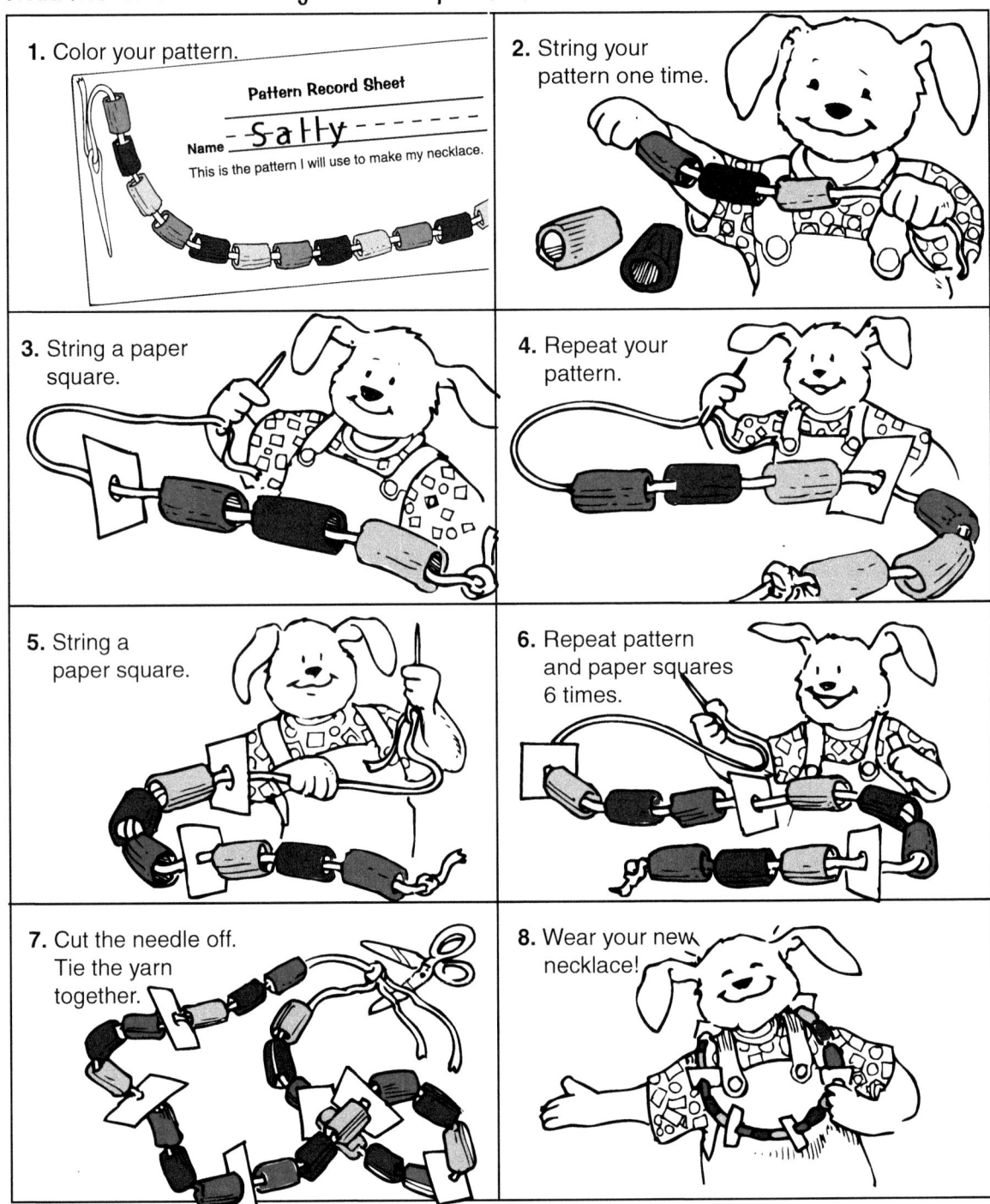

1. Color your pattern.

2. String your pattern one time.

3. String a paper square.

4. Repeat your pattern.

5. String a paper square.

6. Repeat pattern and paper squares 6 times.

7. Cut the needle off. Tie the yarn together.

8. Wear your new necklace!

© Evan-Moor Corp.• EMC 3300

An Experiment

Question:

What will happen when soap is added to a bowl of water and food coloring?

a. The water will turn white.
b. The soap will make bubbles.
c. The food coloring will move in the bowl.
d. The water will begin to make noises.

1. Collect your equipment. You need:
   - a small bowl
   - water
   - food coloring
   - liquid soap
   - ruler

2. Put about a one inch (2.5 cm) of water in the bowl. Let the water sit until it is still.

3. Drop a few spots of food coloring into the bowl very carefully.

4. Slowly pour some liquid soap down the side of the bowl into the water.

5. Watch what happens. Talk about why you think this happens.

6. Clean up your work area.
   - Pour out the water.
   - Wash and dry the bowl.
   - Wipe up any spills.
   - Put materials away.

© Evan-Moor Corp. • EMC 3300

Bird in a Cage

Read all of the instructions. Do the steps one at a time.

1. Lay the template on the tagboard. Trace the square.

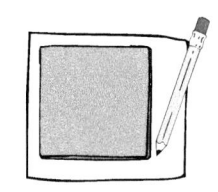

2. Cut out the square.

3. Draw a birdcage on one side of the tagboard.

4. Draw a small bird on the other side. Make the bird in the center of the square.

5. Make a small X on the tagboard under the birdcage.

6. Put a drop of glue on the X. Lay the end of the straw on the glue. Let the glue dry.

7. Spin the straw between your hands. Can you see the bird in its cage?

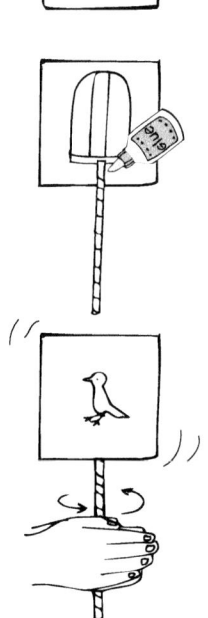

Pennsylvania Facts

written by Luke See

Pennsylvania is one of the oldest states in the United States. In fact, it was the second state **admitted** to the country. Some of the oldest American **colonies** were in Pennsylvania. Back then, only a few thousand people lived there. Today, Pennsylvania has a **population** of more than 12 million people. The city of Harrisburg is the state **capital**. There are several other big cities in Pennsylvania. Philadelphia and Pittsburgh are two of the most popular cities.

Each state in the United States has several official **symbols** and titles. The nickname of Pennsylvania is the Keystone State. The state flower is the mountain laurel. Pennsylvania even has a state food! It is the chocolate chip cookie. Because Pennsylvania is an old state, it has a lot of history. For example, the first American zoo was in Pennsylvania. The state is also home to one of the first radio stations. There is a lot to learn about Pennsylvania.

Glossary

admitted: the act of allowing someone or something to join or enter

capital: the city where the government leaders of a state work

colonies: settlements made by travelers from other countries

population: all the people who live in an area

symbol: an object or word that stands for something else

Works Cited

Thompson, Carol Lewis, and E. Willard Miller. "Pennsylvania." *Encyclopædia Britannica*, 11 Oct. 2018, www.britannica.com/place/Pennsylvania-state. Accessed 14 Dec. 2018.

Fun with Magnets

Magnets have a force. How do we know the force is there? We can see magnets pull things that are made of iron or steel. Magnets have forces that are different strengths. Stronger magnets can pull or move heavier objects. How can you test the force? You can make a game that will show the magnet's force at work. Before you make the game, test the magnet to make sure it is strong enough. First, place the paper clip in the box lid. Hold the magnet below the lid and move it around. If it moves the paper clip, the magnet is strong enough. If it does not, you need a stronger magnet.

Materials: a shoebox lid, 2 sheets of paper, scissors, tape, colored pens, a metal paper clip, a magnet

Make a Magnet Game

1. Trace the shape of the shoebox lid on a sheet of paper. Cut out the traced shape.

2. Draw a flower and a beehive in two corners of the shape. Draw a path with loops and turns, that starts at the beehive and ends at the flower. Place the paper inside the box lid so that you can see the pictures.

3. Draw a bee on paper. Cut it out. Tape the paper clip to the back of the bee. Place the bee at the beehive.

4. Have a friend hold the magnet under the lid and use it to move the bee along the path. The object of the game is to move the bee from the beehive to the flower.

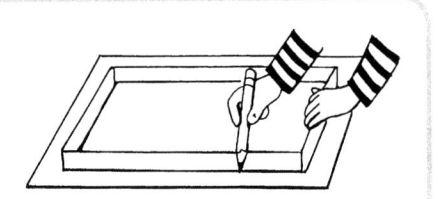

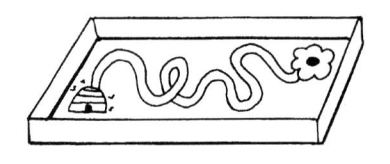

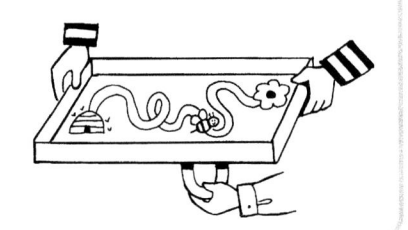

Write a Postcard

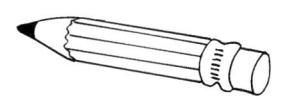

Read how to do it carefully. Follow steps: 1, 2, and 3. . . .

1. Put on the address label.

   My Family
   1234 Home
   Town, State
   00001

2. Put on the stamp.

   My Family
   1234 Home
   Town, State
   00001

3. Turn the postcard over and write.

   Dear Family,
   Can you guess who this card is from?

   You might say:
   Thank you for all the things you do for me.
   I am learning to read directions.
   Isn't it fun to get mail?

4. Color a picture.

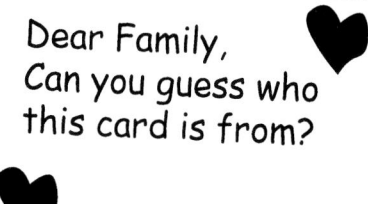

   Dear Family,
   Can you guess who this card is from?

5. Sign the card.

   Dear Family,
   Can you guess who this card is from?
   Love,
   Me

6. Mail the card.

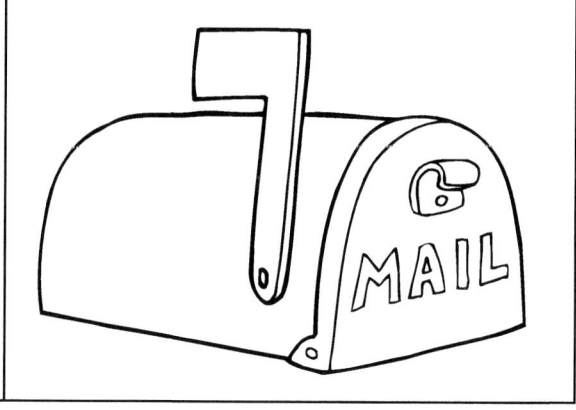

Example Dictionary Page

bat   **brush**

bat (bat), **1.** a wooden stick or club used to hit a ball. **2.** a flying mammal with wings of thin skin. *noun.*

beak (bēk), the bill of a bird. *The bird had a worm in its beak. noun.*

blimp (blimp), a kind of balloon that can be steered. *A blimp is filled with a gas that is lighter than air.* See picture. *noun.*

bliz zard (bliz´ erd), a very cold snowstorm with strong winds. *The blizzard covered our house with snow. noun.*

boil (boil), bubble up and give off steam. *The hot water began to boil. verb.*

bro ken (bro´ ken), in pieces. *The cup was broken. adjective.*

brush (brush), **1.** a tool for cleaning or putting on paint. *noun.* **2.** use a brush on. *I brush my hair until it shines. verb.* **3.** wipe away; remove. *He brushed the tears out of his eyes. verb.*

Example Glossary

Glossary

burrow	a tunnel or an underground home
camouflage	a color or pattern used to hide from danger
dinosaur	a group of reptiles that lived on the earth long ago
endangered	a kind of plant or animal in danger of dying out
fossils	the hardened remains of an animal or a plant from long, long ago
hatch	when a baby animal comes out of its eggshell
nest	a place built by a bird or other animal where it lays its eggs and/or raises its young
predator	an animal that kills other animals for food
prey	an animal that is hunted and eaten by other animals
scales	hard plates covering the body of a reptile
tortoise	a land turtle

The Threat to Polar Bears

written by Luke See
illustrated by Walter Sattazahn

Polar bears live in the Arctic. They tend to live and hunt along shorelines. Their diet mainly consists of the seals that they hunt. The Arctic's cold temperature means there is a lot of ice. Polar bears use this ice to hunt. They wait for seals to come up for air in holes in the ice. Sometimes, they swim below the ice to catch their food. Climate change has had a negative impact on polar bears. Ice is melting earlier every year. This gives polar bears less time to hunt. Less time to hunt means less food for the bears. If things do not change, polar bears could become extinct.

Glossary

Arctic: the areas of land around the North Pole

climate change: the process of the planet heating up over the years

extinct: when an entire type of animal dies out and is gone forever

seal: a sea mammal that uses its flippers to swim and is commonly found in cold regions

temperature: a measure of how hot or cold something is

Works Cited

"Polar Bear." *Encyclopædia Britannica*, kids.britannica.com/kids/article/polar-bear/574591. Accessed 11 Dec. 2018.

"Polar Bear Profile." *National Geographic Kids*, 26 March 2014, kids.nationalgeographic.com/animals/polar-bear/#polar-bear-cub-on-mom.jpg. Accessed 11 Dec. 2018.

Parts of an Apple

Nutritious and juicy, an apple is a sweet treat. An apple has six parts, each with a job to do.

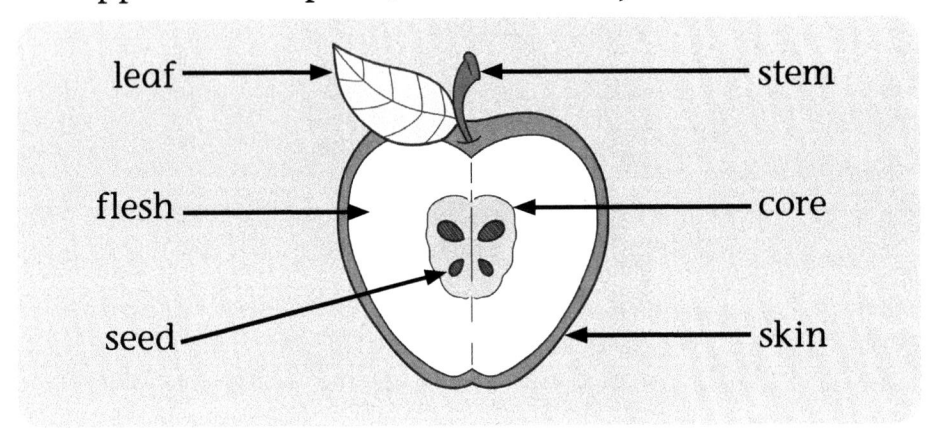

Stem The stem is at the top of the apple. It looks like a tiny twig. The stem has leaves growing from it. It helps the leaves face the sun so they can make food. The stem also holds the apple to the tree.

Leaf An apple leaf is smooth and green on the top. It is fuzzy and silver-green on the bottom. The leaf uses water, sunlight, and air to make food for the tree. Water and air come and go through tiny holes in the leaf. The veins carry water and food to the rest of the tree.

Core The core is at the center of the apple. Its main job is to keep the seeds. Most people do not eat the core, since it has hard seeds.

Parts of an Apple, continued

Skin The skin is smooth and sometimes waxy. It can be green, red, pink, yellow, or a mix of these colors. The skin protects the insides of the apple and keeps it juicy. Did you know that the skin is the most nutritious part of the apple? If you want lots of vitamins, eat the skin!

Flesh The flesh is the best part of the apple. It tastes good! The color of the flesh can be anywhere from snow white to bright red. The flesh is full of water. That is why it is so juicy. This is the part that goes into pie, juice, and applesauce.

Seed A seed is a new apple tree waiting to happen. If you slice an apple across, you will have a circle. See the star in the center? That's the seed pocket. All apples have five seed pockets. The number of seeds in each seed pocket depends on the kind of apple.

Some apple parts are good to eat and some are not. But all six apple parts work together to help the apple grow. They help the apple get big and juicy. Then you can eat it!

Saucy Apple Pudding

Serves 1

Ingredients:
- applesauce
- cinnamon
- chopped nuts*
  (almonds or walnuts)
- crushed pineapple
- whipped topping

Cooking Equipment:
- measuring cup
- can opener
- measuring spoons
- plastic spoon
- small bowl

*Make sure no one is allergic to nuts.

What to Do:

1. Put 1/2 cup of applesauce in a small bowl.

2. Add 1 teaspoon of chopped nuts.

3. Add 2 tablespoons of crushed pineapple.

4. Add a pinch of cinnamon.

5. Stir gently.

6. Add 1 tablespoon of whipped topping.

7. Eat. Yum! Yum!

Instructions for Cooking

1. Wash your hands carefully.

2. Put on an apron.

3. Collect your ingredients from the food table.

4. Collect your utensils from the equipment table.

5. Read the recipe with your group.

6. Decide who is going to do each step.

7. Take the completed food to the serving table.

8. Clean up your work area.

Trail Mix

How to make:
- Place in a muffin cup:
  1 tablespoon raisins
  1 tablespoon banana chips
  1 tablespoon chocolate chips
  1 tablespoon peanuts
- Mix with a stir stick.

Utensils:
muffin cup
tablespoon
stir stick

Make a Stamp for Printing

Materials
- scratch paper
- inner sole
- cardboard
- plastic bottle cap
- construction paper
- stamp pad
- pencil or black marking pen
- glue
- scissors

Steps to Follow
1. Plan your design. Sketch it on scratch paper. Cut out the pattern.
2. Lay your design on the inner sole. Trace around the design.
3. Cut out the design.
4. Glue the design to the cardboard. Write your name on the other side of the cardboard.
5. Glue the bottle cap to the side with your name. This is a handle to help as you make a print.
6. Let the glue dry.
7. Press the stamp on the stamp pad. Make a pattern on the construction paper.

The Best Day of the Weekend

written by Vincent Scotto
illustrated by Sean Ricciardi

Saturday is better than Sunday. Lots of people believe this is true. Many things make Saturday better.

Saturday is great. It is the first day of the weekend. Saturday has the best cartoons on TV. You can wake up early or sleep in. There is plenty of time for fun on Saturday. Saturday is the most fun day of the week!

Sunday is horrible. Kids and adults have to go to bed early. They need to get up for school or work on Monday. Sunday has TV shows for adults. Some kids have to do chores on Sunday. That is no fun! Who would like Sunday over Saturday?

Saturday is better than Sunday. Saturday has all the best parts of a perfect day. Do you believe Saturday is better?

Plants Aplenty

written by Debbie Parrish

Every day, Cathy walked home from kindergarten with her older sister, Pam. On their walk, they always passed the same flower shop. It was called Plants Aplenty Florist. The shop was run by a nice older lady named Mrs. Fragrance. Cathy liked Mrs. Fragrance a lot, even though her name was a bit hard to say. Most times, Cathy just called her "the flower lady."

One day, Pam and Cathy were walking home like usual. But it was not a usual day. It was their mother's birthday! Pam and Cathy had saved up their allowances to buy their mother a present. But they could not agree on what to buy.

"Let's go to the ice cream store," said Pam. "We can pick out an ice cream cake."

Cathy had another idea in mind. "I know!" she said. "Let's go see the flower lady! She could help us pick something for Mom."

"Aw, Cathy, you always want to stop there," said Pam. "I like my idea better. We can get a pretty ice cream cake and write a nice note on it with frosting."

"It's too hot outside," replied Cathy. "The ice cream cake might melt while we're bringing it home. Besides, the flower shop beats the ice cream shop any day of the week."

"What's so great about it?" asked Pam. "It's just a bunch of boring old plants in a room. And they're all the same."

"Flowers are all plants," agreed Cathy. She had learned that in school. "But they are not all the same!"

"They all have leaves, stems, and blossoms," argued Pam. "That seems the same to me."

"But some plants have big leaves and some have small leaves," argued Cathy. "Leaves can be light green or dark green. They can be shiny or really dull. And stems can be different, too! Sometimes there's a thick stem. Sometimes there's a very thin stem. There are tall stems and short stems, and even stems with sharp thorns…yowch! And don't forget—"

"Okay, all right!" Pam cut in with a laugh. "If it means that much to you, we can stop and look at flowers for Mom."

The girls reached the front door to Plants Aplenty. As they went in, Pam and Cathy heard the tinkle of the bell over the door. The bell let Mrs. Fragrance know they were in the shop.

"Well, there's my little friend, the flower girl!" said Mrs. Fragrance. That was her nickname for Cathy. "What brings you young ladies in today?"

"It's our mom's birthday," answered Cathy. "I thought we could get her a present here."

"Well, flowers do make a lovely gift!" said Mrs. Fragrance. "Do you think she would like live flowers or cut flowers?"

"What's the difference?" asked Pam.

"Well, live flowers and cut flowers have different needs," explained Mrs. Fragrance. "Live flowers still have their roots. They need soil, sunlight, and plenty of water to keep growing. Cut flowers are a little easier to handle. They just need water to stay fresh. You can put them in a glass vase to hold them."

"What do you think, Pam?" asked Cathy. "Live or cut?"

"Let's get cut flowers," decided Pam. "They sound like less work."

"Good idea," said Mrs. Fragrance. "There's another good thing about getting cut flowers—you can mix and match the different ones to make a lovely bouquet! Would you like to pick out some colors?"

"You're the flower expert," Pam told Cathy. "You go ahead."

Cathy looked around carefully. "It's so hard to choose my favorite," she finally said. "I love the reds and yellows, but all of the colors are so pretty."

"Let's look around some more," said Mrs. Fragrance. "In the next room, there are many more colors, like pink, purple, and blue."

Mrs. Fragrance showed the girls around. She pointed out her favorite flowers and suggested a few kinds that would look nice together. "It's so nice that you girls are picking out a present for your mother," she said. "Go ahead and pick a dozen flowers. I'll throw in a vase to hold them for free!"

Cathy and Pam smiled. "That is very kind of you, Mrs. Fragrance!" said the older girl. "Cathy, go ahead and pick."

"No, Pam, you do it," answered Cathy. "It's too hard for me. I love them all so much!"

"Okay, then," replied Pam. "Let's start with this long yellow one. Then we'll get two of the short ones with red blossoms, two of the purples…." Pam went on picking flowers until she almost had a dozen. "We can add one with a huge pink blossom," she went on, "and that one with the orange streaks on the petals."

"You're up to eleven flowers," said Mrs. Fragrance. "Cathy, why don't you pick the last flower?"

Cathy peered around the shop. "Aha!" she said. "Let's get the one with the big green leaves and the tiny white flower on top."

"Good choice," said Pam.

Mrs. Fragrance cut the flowers' stems and bunched them together.

"Wow!" exclaimed Pam. "It's so colorful. It almost looks like a rainbow!"

Mrs. Fragrance placed the flower bunch in a tall, clear, glass vase. She put a special red bow on the vase. She told the girls to fill the vase with water as soon as they got home.

Pam paid for the gift and the girls left Plants Aplenty. "You were right," admitted Pam as the sisters walked home. "This is a way better present than an ice cream cake. Mom's going to love it."

"Told you!" said Cathy.

"You did," agreed Pam. "You might be my little sister, but sometimes you know a little more than I do."

Cathy blushed and giggled. "You're silly," she said.

"Flowers really aren't boring at all," said Pam. "There are so many different kinds that it is hard to get tired of looking at them. Still, there is one way that they are all the same."

"Oh yeah?" asked Cathy. "How's that?"

Pam replied with a smile, "Every single one is beautiful!"

The Pumpkin Patch

written by Summer York
illustrated by Dave Rushbrook

The school bus stopped. Everyone cheered. It was the first-grade field trip. The students were thrilled. They were at the pumpkin patch!

The pumpkin patch was on a farm. The farm was huge. There were grassy fields with tall cornstalks.

The teacher stood up. Everyone got quiet. Ms. Morris went over the rules. It is important to follow the rules.

Stay with the group. No running. Listen to the adults. Raise your hand to ask a question. Be careful so you do not get hurt.

They took a hayride. A tractor pulled a big wagon. The wagon was full of soft hay.

The tractor climbed a hill. They were at the pumpkin patch. There were bright orange pumpkins everywhere! Each student picked a pumpkin.

Then they had to go. The wagon took them down the hill. The students climbed off. They walked toward the bus.

Luke wanted to be first. He ran ahead. He tripped. He dropped his pumpkin. It splattered on the ground.

Luke felt bad. He wanted another pumpkin. But it was time to leave. He should have just followed the rules.

A Special Machine

There is a special machine on the planet Mars. It's a rover called *Curiosity*. Where did it come from? It was sent from Earth! Scientists at NASA worked hard to build the *Curiosity Rover*. It left Earth in 2011 and got to Mars in 2012. Ever since then, *Curiosity* has been sending information back to Earth. The rover moves along the surface of Mars. We have learned a lot about Mars from this rover.

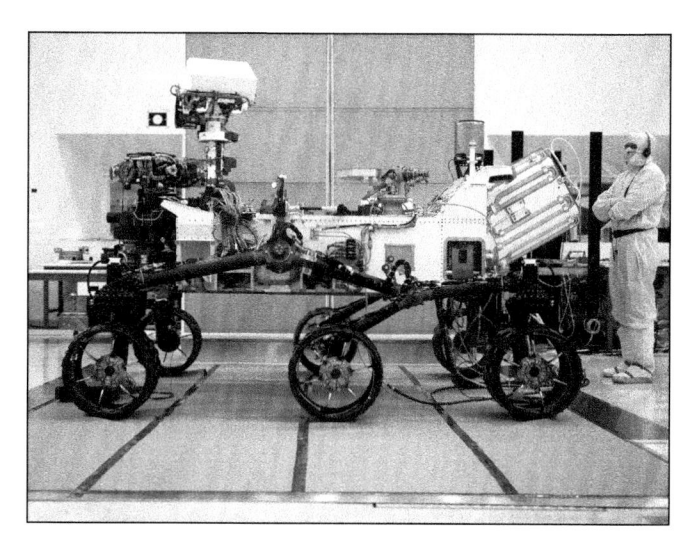

Curiosity was built here on Earth. It went to Mars in a spaceship.

Curiosity uses an arm to pick up rocks and soil. The arm is seven feet long. The rover can pick up a rock with its arm. The arm puts the rock inside the rover. *Curiosity* can study what the rock is made from.

Scientists on Earth tell *Curiosity* what to do. Talking to *Curiosity* is something like playing a video game. From Earth, scientists can see what *Curiosity* is doing. The rover has 17 cameras. It takes a lot of pictures. It sends a lot of information back to Earth!

A Forest Food Chain

Humans need food to stay alive. Food gives us energy. It helps us grow and stay healthy. Animals need food, too. Some animals eat plants. Some animals eat other animals. An animal that eats another animal is a predator. A food chain has animals that depend on each other. Let's look at a forest food chain to see how it works.

This food chain starts with plants. Many plants grow in the forest. An earthworm can eat part of a plant. It can get energy from the plant. A mouse is a predator. A mouse eats the earthworm. The mouse will get energy from the earthworm. The mouse will grow bigger and stronger. But there are many other forest predators that are hungry, too. A fox may catch the mouse. It may eat the mouse for food. Now the fox has energy and it can stay healthy. This is how one kind of forest food chain works.

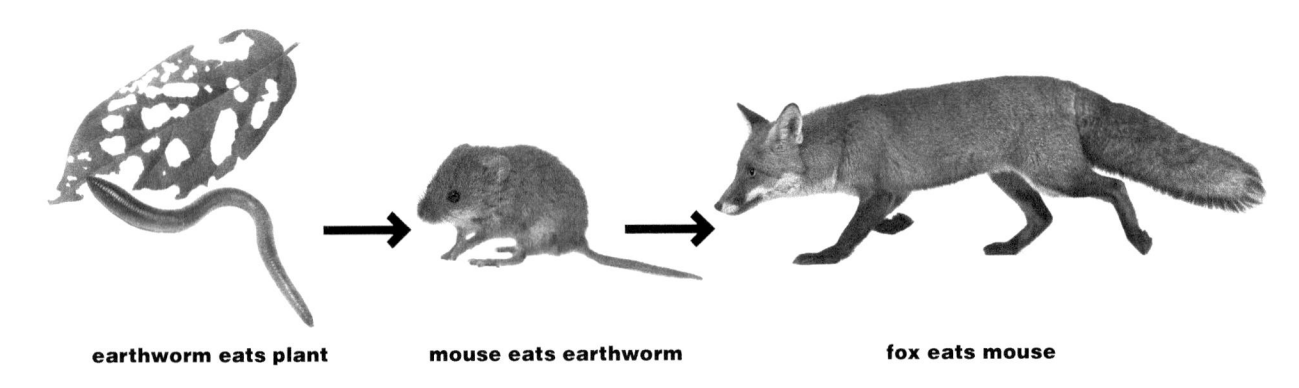

earthworm eats plant → **mouse eats earthworm** → **fox eats mouse**

Doctor's Office

Sometimes, people go to the doctor's office when they are **sick**, or not feeling well. The doctor helps them feel better. When people feel well, they can run, play, and do work. Sometimes, people go to the doctor's office when they feel fine. They visit the doctor to get a checkup.

When you visit the doctor for a checkup, the doctor checks your body to see how much you have grown. The doctor checks your heart. The doctor listens to it beat. The doctor checks your **stomach** because it needs to be healthy. The doctor checks your throat and asks you to say "ahhh." Sometimes, the doctor asks you what foods you eat.

Eating healthy foods can make you feel strong so you can play and do your chores at home. Some foods are not as healthy as others. Unhealthy foods can make you feel **weak**, or too tired to play and work.

Young people, such as babies and children, go to the doctor. Older people, or adults, go to the doctor, too. Visiting the doctor helps many people be healthy.

Beavers at Work

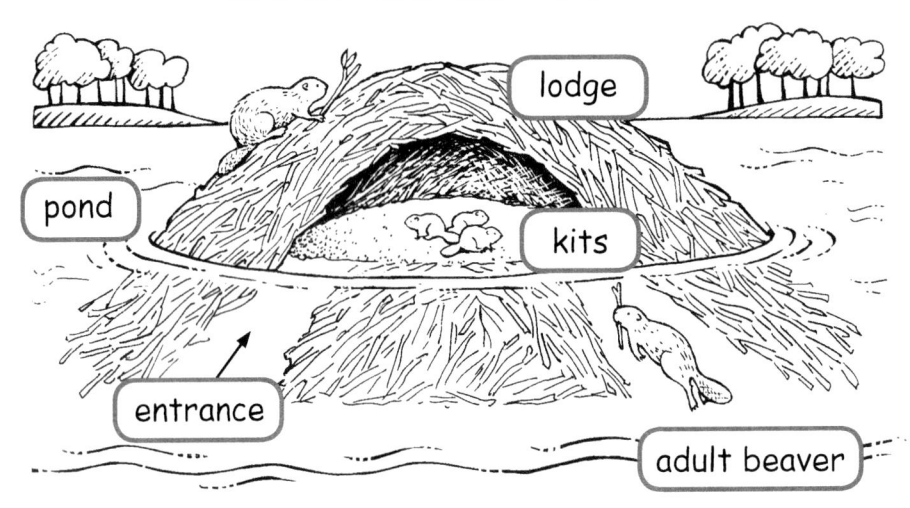

Diagram labels: lodge, pond, kits, entrance, adult beaver

Beavers are very busy animals. When a beaver family moves to a new place, they start working right away. They start by building a dam. A dam stops water from moving down a stream. A dam can change the direction of a stream or make a new pond.

After beavers build a dam, they build special water homes, or lodges. Their bodies help them work well under water. Beavers can close off their nose and ears to keep water out. Their strong back feet are webbed.

Beavers use sticks and grass to build their homes. They also use mud. First, beavers use their sharp front teeth to cut wood. Then they push the wood through the water to the lodge area where they stack the wood. Next, beavers use their claws to scoop up mud and grass. Finally, they pack the mud and grass on top of the lodge. It holds all of the sticks together. The entrance to the lodge is under the water. Beaver lodges help keep beavers safe from other animals.

The Life of a Worker Bee

Most people know that bees have wings. They also know that bees can sting. But did you know that bees have special jobs? The leader of a group of bees is called the queen. The queen bee only has one job. She lays eggs. But worker bees do different jobs as they grow. They work hard to take care of their hives, or homes.

First, a worker bee cleans the cell where it was born. The cell is made of wax. The cell can be used again for a new baby bee. Cells can also be used to store food. Many cells all together are called a honeycomb.

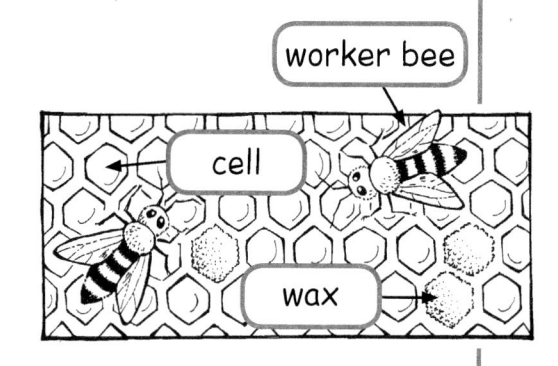

Then, when a worker bee is three days old, it makes food. This food can be royal jelly or worker jelly. The queen is the only bee that gets the royal jelly. The rest of the baby bees eat worker jelly. Worker bees go to each cell to feed the new babies. Hives can have up to 80,000 bees inside of them. Worker bees have to make a lot of food!

Next, when the worker bee is a bit older, it begins to make wax. The wax is used to build new cells. The bees are always trying to make their hive bigger and better.

Finally, when it is three weeks old, the worker bee can fly away from the hive. It looks for food in flowers and fields. It will bring the food back to the hive. There, the workers will make the food into honey. Worker bees have a busy life!

Freshwater Lakes

Freshwater lakes are very important. People and animals need fresh water to live. Plants also need fresh water. There is a lot of water in Earth's oceans. People can't drink ocean water, though. Oceans have salt water. That's not the kind of water that people and animals drink.

Freshwater lakes get their water in different ways. One way they get water is from melting snow. The snow is on the tops of mountains. When the snow melts, the water goes into rivers. Some of these rivers run into lakes.

Rivers and lakes have fresh water for insects and other animals to drink. There is fresh water for certain kinds of fish to live in. People take fresh water from the lakes, too. They run pipes from the lakes into their towns or cities. Now there is water for people to drink!

Making a New Lake

People and animals use lakes in many different ways. Cities and towns use lakes to get drinking water. People play and swim in lakes. Lakes are homes for some kinds of fish. Insects and other animals also drink from lakes. Water is very important to all living things.

Freshwater lakes are important to people because people shouldn't drink salt water. It will make them very sick. Only a small number of lakes have salt water in them. Salt water is also in Earth's oceans.

So what do people do if they don't have a freshwater lake close to them? They can make one! These kinds of lakes are called man-made lakes. Some are made by dams. Others are made by taking water from a river. People use machines to dig a large hole. Then they make the river flow into the hole. There will be a new freshwater lake for everyone to enjoy.

Before **During** **After**

Learning from Pictures

Photography is the art of taking pictures, or photographs, with a camera. There are many kinds of photographers. Some photographers take photographs of people. Some take photographs of things in the news. Still others photograph tiny cells in a science lab.

picture on a cellphone

pictures printed on photo paper

There are many kinds of cameras, too. Some use film. Some use digital photo cards. All cameras work in the same basic way. They take in light and focus it into images. The cameras record, or keep, those images. People can print the pictures on special photo paper. They can also look at digital photographs on computers. Many people take photographs and look at them on cellphones.

Credit: ESA/Hubble & NASA

This photograph shows the nearest star to our sun. This star is many trillions of miles away.

Photography is a useful technology. A space telescope takes photographs of objects in space that are very far away. High-speed cameras take photographs of things that happen too quickly for human eyes to see. Old photographs show what life was like in the past. Photography helps people learn about the past, the present, and even the future.

What Cameras Can Do

Camera pictures can show us things we can't see every day. Special cameras can go places where people can't go. Some cameras go deep into the oceans. The underwater cameras take pictures of animals that live in very deep water. Humans can't go that deep, but cameras can. We can see amazing fish and other sea creatures.

A diver uses an underwater camera to take pictures of fish near the bottom of the ocean.

Tiny cameras can go inside the human body. These cameras can help doctors. The pictures can show why someone is sick. One small camera can go inside a person's ear. The doctor can take a picture. The picture will show the inside of the ear. This can help the doctor learn why the person has an earache. Cameras are useful and help us learn many things.

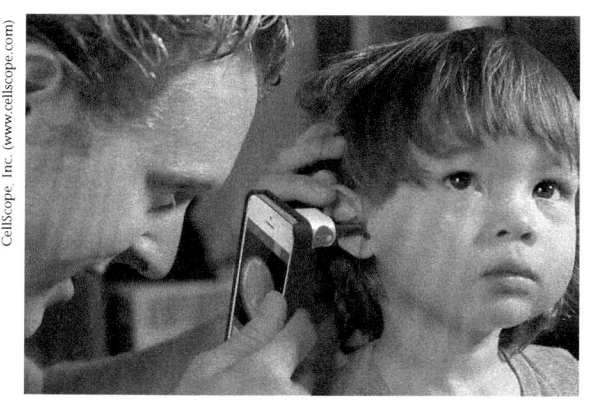

The doctor uses the camera to look in the child's ear for an ear infection.

A Promise and a Prince

written by Luke See
illustrated by Brittanie Markham

There once was a young prince who was selfish. He always broke his promises to the people of the kingdom. One day, an old wizard decided he had had enough of the prince's selfish ways. He came to the castle and, in the blink of an eye, cast a spell. The young prince was turned into a frog! "Now you must count on the kindness of others," said the wizard. "You will stay a frog until a promise is made to you and kept."

The frog prince hopped down the hall. He saw the baker and tried to call for help. Before he could even speak, the baker shrieked at the sight of him. He picked up the frog prince and threw him outside the castle.

Now, the frog prince realized he did not know where to go. He hopped and hopped for miles. He came upon a young princess crying next to a well.

"What is the matter, little one?" the frog prince asked.

"My golden ball has fallen down the well. I cannot reach it!"

"I will get you your ball. But you have to promise to take me home and show me some kindness," the frog prince said. Secretly, he hoped that the princess might break the curse.

"Oh, yes, I promise!" said the princess. However, as soon as the frog prince got the princess her ball, she ran back to her castle without him. She broke her promise, just as he had many times before.

The frog prince followed after her. He hopped and hopped and hopped. Finally, he reached the castle door. He knocked until the king answered. The king was the young princess's father. The frog explained how he had helped. He told the king of the princess's promise.

"This will not do," said the king. "She must do as she promised."

The king carried the frog prince into the dining hall. He sat him down next to the princess and ordered her to share her food. The princess was surprised. At first, she acted very annoyed. But her father explained to her the importance of keeping her promise. By the time dessert was served, she even fed the frog a few bites of cake.

When it came time for bed, the king told her to share her room. The princess protested. She did not want a slimy frog touching her things. The king again reminded her of her promise. Finally, the princess agreed. She took a comfy pillow and placed a small cloth down like a blanket.

The frog prince was very happy. The kindness of the princess and the comfort of the pillow made him forget all about the curse. He fell fast asleep. When he awoke, he found himself sprawled out on the floor. He had turned back into himself. He jumped to his feet and shouted with joy. The princess and the king were very surprised.

"I was under a spell," he said. "I had to remain a frog until someone kept their promise to me!"

The king was happy that his daughter had learned to keep her promise. The princess was even happier that she did not have to share her room or food with a frog!

The Boy Who Cried Wolf

An Aesop Fable

A shepherd boy was in charge of tending a flock of sheep. Every morning he took the sheep to a meadow near his village. Every evening he brought the sheep back home. All day long he watched the sheep to make sure they were not harmed or didn't wander off and get lost.

One day the shepherd boy began to complain. "I am bored," he said. "There is nothing to do but watch these silly sheep eat grass. Nothing different ever happens." As he watched the sheep munching on the tall green grass, he had an idea. What fun it would be to fool the villagers. He would pretend that a wolf was attacking the flock of sheep.

"Wolf! Wolf!" he shouted. The villagers came running with pitchforks and clubs to drive off the wolf. When they arrived there was no wolf. There was just the naughty shepherd boy laughing his head off.

Again and again, the shepherd boy called wolf. Again and again the villagers came. Each time there was no wolf.

At last, one day, a hungry wolf crept up on the flock. When the shepherd boy saw the wolf, he began to shout, "Wolf! Wolf!" He shouted and shouted, but no one came. The villagers thought the boy was up to his old tricks, so they ignored his calls. The wolf killed sheep after sheep before the boy finally drove it away.

The shepherd boy finally learned that no one believes a liar even when he is telling the truth.

© Evan-Moor Corp. • EMC 757

The Patient Wolf

written by Luke See
illustrated by Sean Ricciardi

A hungry wolf came out of the woods. He saw a small shepherd with a large flock of sheep. The wolf licked his lips. He wanted a tasty sheep or two for dinner. The wolf sneaked around the village and saw many people. He was afraid he might be attacked if he tried to eat a sheep. The wolf went back into the woods to plot his next move. A few moments later, he heard the shepherd boy cry out.

"Wolf! Wolf!" the boy shouted. The wolf was startled. Surely he had not been seen. He looked closely, but there was no other wolf to be seen. The sheep were all safe. After a few minutes, dozens of farmers had gathered with weapons at the ready. The shepherd boy started to laugh at the farmers.

"I tricked you!" he said, continuing to laugh. "There is no wolf!" The farmers all turned and left. None of them joined in the laughter. The wolf saw this joke as an opportunity. He licked his lips again. The young prankster had given him a good idea.

The wolf waited near the flock for days. He hid in the woods. Sure enough, the shepherd boy played the same trick, day after day. Each day, the farmers gathered their weapons and the boy laughed at them. As the days passed, however, fewer and fewer farmers came to help. Finally, it was time. The wolf was too hungry to wait any longer.

He attacked the flock. He ate up sheep after sheep. The shepherd boy called out, "Wolf! Wolf!" Nobody came to stop the wolf. He ate until his stomach was full. When he was done, he ran off into the woods. The wolf could not believe his luck. It was the easiest meal of his life!

Big Pig and the Pancake

written by Luke See
illustrated by Walter Sattazahn

Of all the animals on the farm, Big Pig was the smartest. Dull Donkey could not keep up. Chester Chicken had no patience. The animals all lived together at the base of a hill. Everyone knew that Big Pig was the boss.

At the top of the hill lived a family. There was an old woman and seven loud children. Big Pig did not care much for humans. But there was one thing he loved. Twice a day, he could smell the old woman's cooking. The smell of her meals floated down the hill. Each time it hit Big Pig's nose, his belly grumbled. He daydreamed about having a bite for himself.

One day, his luck changed. Big Pig heard a loud commotion from up on the hill. A huge pancake came rolling out of the house. The old woman and her seven children chased it outside. The pancake rolled too fast, and it soon bounced down the hill. It came to a stop in front of Dull Donkey to ask for help.

"Hold still, pancake," Dull Donkey said. "I can't eat you if you roll so fast."

"I ran away from the old woman and her children," the pancake said. "I will run from you too." He rolled away, going farther down the hill. Next, the pancake rolled toward Chester Chicken. Before he could even stop to ask for help, the chicken attacked. The pancake saw him coming and rolled right past.

Finally, the pancake got to the edge of the farm. It rolled to a stop in front of Big Pig.

"Good day, Pancake," said Big Pig.

"The same to you, Big Piggy," said the pancake.

"This farm isn't safe for you, Pancake," said Big Pig. "Let's travel together. I'll get you safely to the forest."

The pancake thanked Big Pig. The two traveled toward the forest. Soon, they came to a small stream. Big Pig jumped in and began to swim across.

"Wait for me, Big Pig," the pancake said. "I cannot swim."

"No problem," answered Big Pig. "Sit here on my snout and I'll carry you over."

Without thinking, the pancake jumped in the air toward Big Pig's snout. At the last second, Big Pig opened his mouth and swallowed the pancake whole.

"Delicious!" said Big Pig. It turns out the old woman on the hill was a great cook after all!

How the Princess Learned to Laugh
A Folktale from Poland

There once was a princess who never laughed. Her father, the king, was worried about his daughter. He promised her hand in marriage to any young man who could make her laugh.

A king in a nearby country had two sons. He thought that his elder son was clever, but that his younger son was a fool. Each of his sons wanted to try to make the princess laugh so he could marry her.

The elder son, who was proud and selfish, took a court jester's rattle and cap and set off on his journey. He was sure he would make the princess laugh and would then marry her.

The prince stopped to eat his midday meal near a well. An old man came up to the prince. He asked, "Can you spare a little bread for a hungry traveler?" The selfish prince chased the old man away with his horsewhip.

When the prince arrived at the castle, he put on the jester's cap and stood before the princess. He shook the rattle, did a little dance, and made funny faces. She didn't smile. He told jokes. She didn't smile. He turned cartwheels and stood on his head. Nothing he did made the princess even crack a smile. He had to return home a failure.

When the younger son heard that his brother had failed, he set off to try. He too met the old man when he stopped at the well to eat his midday meal. When the old man asked for some bread, the kind prince gladly shared what he had.

"Bless you, friend!" the old man said. They ate their meal together, then the young prince settled down to take a nap.

While he slept, the young prince had a strange dream. In his dream the old man was an angel sent to Earth to find someone kind. When the prince awoke, he saw a strange sight. There stood a golden coach shaped like a pumpkin. The coach was pulled by a goose and a gander. The coachman was a cross-eyed dog.

The young prince climbed into the coach and started off to the castle. Along the way people pointed and laughed at the strange coach. It was too late to go to the castle that day, so the young prince stopped at an inn, leaving the coach in the inn's courtyard.

The next morning, the innkeeper's greedy wife came into the courtyard. She began to cut gold off the coach with a large kitchen knife. "Oh, no!" she cried. "I'm stuck to the coach." She pulled and pulled, but she couldn't get free.

The young prince didn't see her as he got into the coach. Off he went to the castle, with the innkeeper's wife running along behind. Along the way people tried to pull her off the coach, but they got stuck, too. Soon,

> the innkeeper's wife was stuck to the coach,
>
> a baker was stuck to the innkeeper's wife,
>
> a washerwoman was stuck to the baker, and
>
> a soldier was stuck to the washerwoman.

As the coach reached the castle, people crowded around laughing at the ridiculous parade running behind.

The princess came to see what all the noise was about. Suddenly, the crowd heard a sound they had never heard before. It was the princess laughing harder than anyone! The next day the princess and the kind prince were married. And the princess was never sad again.

Two Princes

written by Luke See
illustrated by Mallory Senich

There once was a kingdom with two princes. Prince Henry was the oldest. He was handsome, tall, and strong. One day he would be king. However, he was also selfish and full of himself. His younger brother was Prince David. David did not care much for being a prince. He spent his time with the townspeople. David was a bit of a daydreamer.

One day their father, the king, came to the two princes. "Princess Penelope, of the kingdom of Lanchester, is looking to marry," the king said. "Her father claims that she will choose whoever can come to court and make her laugh."

"She is as good as mine!" Prince Henry said. He immediately began to get ready for the trip.

"Might I go along too, father?" Prince David asked. "I should love to see the country of Lanchester. I would also be honored to meet the princess."

The king waved David away. "This is no task for you," he said. "You're a fool with your head in the clouds. Be gone so I can help your brother pack."

And so, Prince Henry rode to Lanchester. Prince David remained behind. The king waited for news from his son. As the days passed, no news came. After a week, Prince Henry returned in a foul mood.

"No one will ever marry that woman!" Henry complained. "I danced and sang, I joked and japed. I even dressed up as a jester and did cartwheels. She barely even looked up from her book!"

The king thought long and hard. Then, he ordered Prince David to travel to meet the princess. It took David several days to reach Lanchester. Along the way, he stopped and met strangers. He shared his food with people who were down on their luck. He gave away most of his royal clothing. He even gave his shoes to a young boy. There were so many people he wanted to help. By the time he reached the princess's castle, he wore only his underclothes and his crown.

As Prince David walked into the court, Princess Penelope looked up from her book. She immediately cracked a smile while looking at Prince David's ridiculous outfit. The prince was nervous now. He realized he truly looked like a fool. He tried to walk faster to reach the princess, but he wore no shoes! Just as he reached her throne, Prince David slipped on his socks and toppled to the ground. His crown flew off his head and landed flat on his stomach as he lay on his back.

The princess burst into a fit of laughter! All of the people gathered around joined in. Princess Penelope got to her feet and helped David to his. She placed his crown back on his head.

"I have surely never met a prince like you, sir," Princess Penelope said to Prince David as she grabbed his hand. It seemed that the princess had found her prince.

A Famous Statue

The Statue of Liberty welcomes people who are coming to the United States. The statue holds a torch to light the way for visitors. The Statue of Liberty is community art. It belongs to everyone in the United States. It's a very special statue. It is a symbol of freedom.

The Statue of Liberty was a gift from the people of France. It was built on Liberty Island. The island is in New York Harbor. Millions of people visit the statue every year. The woman in the statue is holding a tablet. The tablet has a date on it. It is written in Roman numerals. The date is July 4, 1776. This date is the birthday of the United States. The statue was a present for the country's 100th birthday.

The Statue of Liberty stands on a concrete and stone wall. The wall is shaped like a star. There is a museum inside. Together, the statue and the base are 305 feet (93 meters) tall. The statue has been holding her torch high to welcome all visitors who come to see her.

The Statue of Liberty's tablet reads: July IV MDCCLXXVI. The letters are Roman numerals that stand for July 4, 1776.

A Gift of Art

The Statue of Liberty is community art. It is for everyone to enjoy. The statue was made by an artist named Frederic Bartholdi. An engineer named Gustave Eiffel helped Bartholdi to make his statue strong. These two men lived in France. The people of France gave the statue to the people of the United States. It is a symbol of freedom and friendship.

People can go to Liberty Island to see the statue. The island is in New York Harbor. The woman in the statue holds a torch. She also holds a tablet. The tablet says July 4, 1776, in Roman numerals. This is the birthday of the United States.

The Statue of Liberty stands on a wall shaped like a star. There is a crown on Liberty's head. There are broken chains near her feet to show she is free. The statue faces southeast. This is so it can face the ships coming into the harbor. The Statue of Liberty welcomes people to the United States.

People can buy special tickets to visit the crown. They have to climb 377 steps inside the statue to get to the crown.

How a Food Chain Works

A caterpillar eats a leaf.

A frog eats a caterpillar.

A snake eats a frog.

A hawk eats a snake.

Food Chain Facts

All living things need food to survive. Many animals eat plants. Animals can also eat other kinds of animals. Animals that eat other animals are predators. Eating food gives animals energy and helps them stay healthy. Food helps animals grow bigger and stronger. If they eat well, animals can live long lives, but many habitats can be dangerous places to live.

Many plants and animals are linked together in food chains. A food chain is a group of plants and animals that get energy from each other. Let's look at how one forest food chain works.

This forest has many plants. An ant eats part of a plant. A frog is the ant's predator. The frog eats the ant. However, the frog has a predator, too. There is a snake waiting to eat the frog. What will eat the snake? An eagle is soaring above and searching for food. It sees the snake and dives down to grab it. Now the food chain is complete, and the eagle is the top predator.

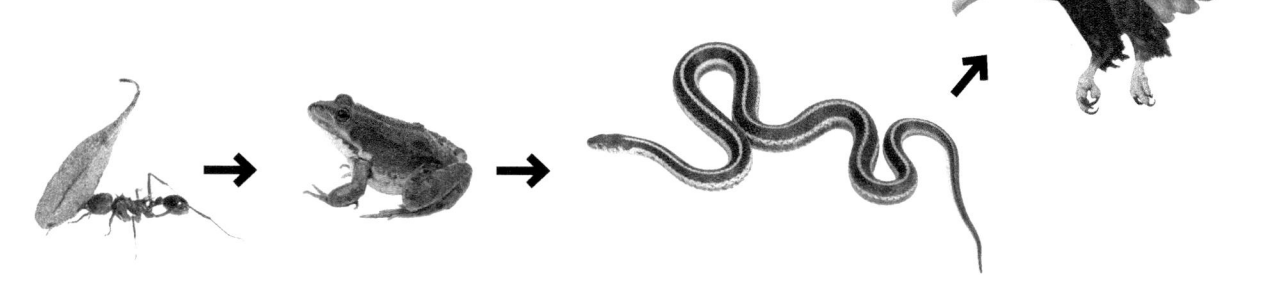

Earthworms in the Garden

Earthworms live in the soil under the ground. Their bodies help them live there. An earthworm's body is made up of many segments, or rings. It has four pairs of stiff hairs called bristles under most of its segments. These hairs help the worm hold onto the soil as it moves through it. Some people like to have earthworms in their gardens because earthworms help to keep the soil healthy. Healthy soil helps plants grow.

Here's how earthworms change the soil to help plants grow. First, they dig large burrows. The burrows let water and air into the soil. Second, earthworms drag dead leaves and plant bits into the burrow and eat them. The food passes through the worm's body. It is left in piles on top of the ground. The soil gets nutrients from the piles. The nutrients help the plants grow.

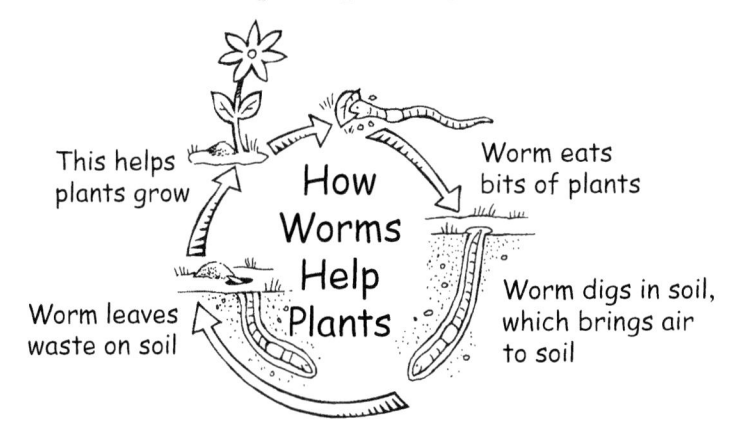

How Worms Help Plants
- This helps plants grow
- Worm eats bits of plants
- Worm digs in soil, which brings air to soil
- Worm leaves waste on soil

You can often see earthworms after it rains. This is because their burrows fill up with water. Gardeners are happy to see the earthworms. They know the worms are helping their gardens grow!